Trees and Shrubs
of New England

Down East Books / Camden / Maine 04843

Other Books By Marilyn Dwelley
Spring Wildflowers of New England
Summer & Fall Wildflowers of New England

Library of Congress Catalogue Card Number
79-52448
ISBN Number 0-89272-064-6

Trees and Shrubs of New England

By Marilyn Dwelley

With a foreword by Dr. Fay Hyland

ACKNOWLEDGMENTS

I would like to express my appreciation to several who have been especially helpful to me in this endeavor.

Dr. Fay Hyland, University of Maine Botany Department who shared with me his expertise on the willows and helped me with the identification, research, and drawing of that very difficult genus; and for his helpful suggestions and encouragements with the rest of the book; and especially for the long hours spent in making a critical review of the entire book.

Dr. Charles Richards, University of Maine Botany Department, who checked my work for botanical accuracy and made many fine suggestions.

Dr. Auburn E. Brower, Augusta, Maine who worked for the state forestry department before his retirement, who helped me greatly in locating the rarer shrubs and trees of Maine. Without his knowledge of the stations for certain species, I would still be searching for specimens.

Lawrence Newcomb, Sharon, Massachusetts (author of his own wildflower guide) who supplied me with many living specimens of shrubs and trees of Massachusetts.

Garret Van Wart of Milton, Massachusetts who willingly collected and provided me with living specimens of shrubs and trees of Massachusetts.

And my friends in the Josselyn Botanical Society who so readily shared their knowledge and training with me and helped me with identification.

Thank you all, from the bottom of my heart!

Marilyn J. Dwelley

PREFACE

Introduction

This book contains most woody plants which grow in New England naturally, and those which were introduced long ago and have become naturalized. Some of the most commonly planted street and lawn trees have been included, but space does not allow inclusion of all horticultural introductions. In general, a woody plant should have a perennial, woody stem which increases in diameter and length each year. Thus, the size of the plant is not the determining factor, and the book includes plants from one inch in height to more than 100 feet in height.

The distinction between a shrub and tree is somewhat difficult — especially in the immature stages. Usually a tree has a single, distinct trunk which supports a crown made up of lateral branches. Shrubs are those woody plants which — at maturity — are less than twenty feet in height and have several main stems or an irregular branching habit. Low plants with tough, slightly-woody stems are difficult to classify. Some may be classified as an herb by some authors and a shrub by others. Many of these questionable species have been included, but others may have been omitted. These will be found in the wildflower books by the author of this publication.

Descriptions and Illustrations

A good illustration is obviously helpful in identification, but more is needed to make positive identification. The reader should study the illustration and read the description before making up his mind. The picture alone is usually not enough. *Key points in identification are in Italics* and careful attention should be given to these. The description of most species will tell the range, habitat, and growth habit. If the reader will note where the plant grows, he can quickly eliminate many similar plants which might not occur in the area where he found his specimen.

The text also includes descriptions of the leaf, flower, fruit, winter buds, and wood whenever possible. These are the most trustworthy characteristics to use. Bark descriptions are sometimes given, but because bark differs greatly with the age of the tree, it is not a reliable characteristic to use.

Rarely — if ever — will one find the leaves, winter buds, flowers, and fruits on the plant all at the same time. Nearly all of the illustrations in this book were drawn from real specimens and depict the plant as it appeared when collected. When possible, other special features have been added, but it was not possible to travel to the site of each plant during each season. If the plant you wish to identify is not in the same stage of growth as the illustration, be sure to read the entire description before attempting to identify it.

There is no scale of drawing included, because it varies with each plant. The drawings of smaller plants will be life-size, while those of larger trees will be greatly reduced. Actual measurements — in most cases — will be given in the text.

Several of the genera have many species with similar characteristics and the minute differences are not easily shown in drawings — (For example, those of *Vaccinium, Crataegus, Salix,* and *Amelanchier*). For this reason, complete drawings may not accompany each description. Sometimes only the distinctive characteristic will be shown; other times there will be no drawing at all if a plant is very similar to the preceding one. The characteristics to use in identification will be given in the text.

Technical and Common Names

The technical names and the order of arrangement follow that of *Gray's Manual of Botany*, 8th ed., 1950 by M.L. Fernald. Occasionally a second Latin name — which is used in other texts — is listed for the convenience of those who wish to compare plant descriptions in several different texts. If there are several common names given to the same plant, the author has included most of them — usually with the most commonly-used one first.

The initials and names after the Latin names stand for the author of that particular species. These are very helpful for botanists, but are of little value to beginners. They have been included for the sake of authenticity.

Personal Note

Many people who have used my two wildflower books have urged me to also write and illustrate one on the shrubs and trees. This has been a major undertaking as I did not know them as well as the flowers. I sincerely hope this book will help those who use it to learn as much as I have learned by doing it.

Marilyn J. Dwelley

FOREWORD

There are thousands of different kinds of plants which may be found growing in any one section of the country. No one person knows all of them. Technically trained botanists have concentrated their efforts on naming and classifying these plants and recording them in books. The descriptions are necessarily detailed and technical and, for the most part, incomprehensible to the layman. These floras are, of course, valuable and indeed indispensable, to botanists, foresters, horticulturists, and others who must know precisely the material with which they are dealing. However, the layman lacks the training and skill to use technical manuals. Illustrations and simple terms are more useful. A book is needed which will aid in the identification of woody plants in wooded areas, fields, or around the home. The text should be comprehensive enough to include all the specimens encountered locally but not so exhaustive as to be cumbersome.

Although several books are devoted to the flora of New England many of them are too specialized, technical, or inclusive to be of value to those with no botanical training or knowledge. By limiting the text to a reasonably well defined area and flora, much time in identification may be saved, and accuracy enhanced. For instance, several kinds of oaks are native to the eastern United States, but only a small percent of them are found in New England. By including only those found in the area of interest, many kinds of oaks are immediately eliminated and will not have to be considered in the text.

Others in addition to the local residents of an area are also interested in the woody plants found there. Tourists and friends from distant places visit the area and are immediately confronted with unfamiliar trees and shrubs.

They are interested in their identification and turn to local book shops and book sections in department stores for suitable texts. Books and local tree guides will be examined by quickly thumbing through the pages before selecting the one best suited for their need. People are color conscious, and the book which has colored illustrations, uses simple language, is pocket size, and appears to contain all the kinds of woody plants in the area, is likely to be considered most informative and valuable.

Certain groups of plants, namely the willows, will serve as an example of the coverage in this book. Most texts describe only a few kinds of willows and skip the others. This author figures and describes practically all of them in the area covered. Willows are a difficult group of plants to identify but the author has put special emphasis on this group because it has been so poorly represented in most texts. The fine colored plates and accompanying descriptions should lend confidence to those who genuinely seek to learn these commonly neglected plants.

This text by Marilyn J. Dwelley, titled *Trees and Shrubs of New England* appears to admirably fill the needs of anyone interested in the identification of woody plants in the New England area. Nearly all of the woody flora is illustrated in natural color, accompanied by a brief, but concise, non-technical description of each specimen. In addition, other useful information is often included. Its durable cover and convenient size enhance the book as a field manual. It should be a delight to own this text. It can advantageously be used in conjunction with *Spring Wildflowers of New England* and *Summer and Fall Wildflowers of New England* — two other books by the author.

Fay Hyland

GLOSSARY

achene	a small, dry, hard, one-celled and one-seeded fruit which does not split open along definite lines at maturity
acute	sharp-pointed without tapering sides
alternate	refers to leaves, buds, or leaf scars when they occur singly different points along the twig
ament	a curved, dry or scaly spike of immature flowers — usually containing flowers of one sex only.
anther	the pollen-bearing part of the stamen
appressed	closely pressed against
axil	the upper angle formed where the leaf is attached to the stem
basal	located at the base of the plant
berry	a simple fleshy or pulpy fruit, usually containing many seeds, but with no central core and no stone (pit)
bloom	a whitish powdery covering, often waxy in nature
bract	a somewhat modified leaf which occurs below a flower, a leaf, or a flower cluster
branchlet	persistent growth of the past few years, excluding the growth of the previous growing season, which is the twig
bristle	a stiff, strong hair—not as strong as a prickle
bud	a rudimentary twig or growing point containing undeveloped vegetative or floral parts, in many cases protected by scales
bundle scars	scars or marks found within the leaf scar which were formed when the leaf fell off
calyx	the outer whorl of flower parts (usually sepals) which sometimes remain on the tip of the fruit
capsule	a dry, many-seeded fruit which splits open along several predetermined valves or cracks when it reaches maturity
catkin	an overwintering structure on some trees which contains immature male or female flowers
chambered	when the pith inside the twig is broken into cavities by evenly-spaced horizontal partitions
compound	when a leaf is divided into separate blades or leaflets
conifer	cone-bearing woody plant

corolla	a collective term for the whorl of petals on a flower
cyme	a broad or flat-topped cluster with the central or terminal flowers blooming the earliest
deciduous	refers to trees whose leaves fall off in autumn
drupe	a simple fleshy fruit with usually one or a few stony pits in the center
elliptic	when something tapers uniformly toward both rounded ends and is broadest in the middle
entire	without teeth or lobes
follicle	a simple, dry fruit which opens along one side at maturity to discharge the seeds
fruit	the seed-bearing organ of a plant
gland or glandular	a secreting surface or structure
habit	the general appearance or manner of growth of a plant
habitat	the type of environment in which a plant grows most frequently
hip	the apple-like fruits of the rose; a receptacle which forms an urn-shaped structure which encloses the bony achenes
inflorescence	the flowering or fruiting portion of a plant
leaf scar	the scar left on a twig after the leaf has fallen; it contains one or more bundle scars
lenticel	a small corky mark on the outside of bark on twigs and branchlets
midrib	the central or main rib of a leaf or leaflet
node	the point on the twig which normally bears one or more leaves
nutlet	a small, hard, dry, one-seeded fruit like a small nut
opposite	when two leaves occur in a pair directly across the twig from each other
ovary	the base of the pistil which holds the ovules that will become seeds
panicle	a flower cluster in which side branches rebranch
pedicel	the stalk which supports a single flower
penduncle	the primary flower stalk supporting a cluster of flowers
petiole	the stalk of a leaf
pith	the central region of a twig—usually spongy and clearly contrasting with the surrounding tissue in texture
pistil	the female part of a flower (see illustration)
pistillate	refers to a flower containing only pistils and no male organs

pollen	spores or grains borne by the anther (tip of the stamen) which fertilizes the ovules in the pistil
pome	a fleshy fruit, such as an apple, which has a core in the center
prickle	a weak, slender, sharp outgrowth on the bark—usually scattered at irregular intervals and not at the nodes only
prostrate	lying flat on the ground
receptacle	an expanded portion at the tip of the flower stalk upon which the flower is borne
samara	a dry, winged fruit
scale	a modified leaf or bract which often covers buds
scurfy	covered by minute scale-like or bran-like particles
seed	the ripened ovule consisting of the embryo and seed coats
sepal	a division of the calyx (see illustration)
sessile	attached without a stalk, directly to the stem
shrub	a woody perennial, smaller than a tree, usually with several stems rather than a single trunk
sinus	the space between two adjacent lobes on a leaf
simple	when a leaf has only one blade and is not compounded into separate leaflets
spine	a sharp, wooden outgrowth of the stem—smaller than a thorn and not occuring at axils
stamen	the male part of the flower (see illustration)
staminate	refers to a flower which contains stamens only and no female organs
stipule	an appendage at the base of the leaf or leaf stalk, quite often in pairs, one on each side of its insertion in the stem
strobile	a cone-like fruiting structure with overlapping bracts or scales covering the seeds
style	the part of the pistil which connects the stigma and the ovary. On some flowers, the style protrudes from the throat of the flower.
subshrub	a barely or only slightly woody plant or shrub
tendril	a slender, long, usually coiling, modification of a leaf or twig tip by which a plant grasps an object and clings to it for support
thorn	a sharp, rigid, spine-like twig or branchlet distinguished from prickles or spines by its greater size and its position in the axil of a leaf scar

tree	a woody plant potentially exceeding twenty feet in height, usually with a single trunk and a definite crown
twig	the growth of the previous growing season. It can be determined by progressing down the stem from the tip to the first abrupt change in color and texture. This point is usually marked by scars from the tip bud of the previous winter.
vein	the thread of fibrovascular tissue in a leaf blade. Veins quite often form a regular pattern or network.
vine	a plant which climbs upon another plant or upon some object by twining or by using tendrils or aerial rootlets
whorled	occurring three or more at one node on the twig

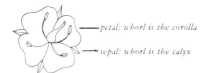

petal; whorl is the corolla

sepal; whorl is the calyx

prickles

thorns

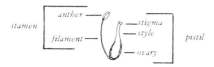

stamen

anther

filament

stigma

style

ovary

pistil

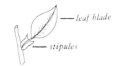

leaf blade

stipules

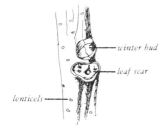

winter bud

leaf scar

lenticels

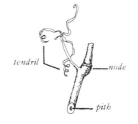

tendril

node

pith

AMERICAN YEW or
GROUND HEMLOCK
Taxus canadensis Marsh.
Yew Family

American Yew is a low straggling shrub which grows in shady, wet, or rocky woods, especially under other evergreens. Yew usually grows in clumps and is commonly 2-3 feet in height, but occasionally reaches heights of nearly five feet.

The very dark green needles have sharp points at the tips and are on short stalks which continue down the smooth twig for a distance below the needles. The underside of the needle is *a warm yellow-green* or lighter green, but it is never whitish or silvery like the needles on the true hemlocks. Needles vary in length from ⅜ to 1 inch.

Insignificant flowers develop in April and May, but the fruit which develops in late summer is very beautiful. It is a clear, bright-red, translucent berry-like cone. The cup-like cone encloses a visible green seed and is about ¼ inch in diameter. The pulp is said to be sweet and edible, but the seed inside is poisonous. The seeds and wilted foliage of the yew are fatal to livestock.

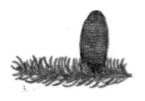

BALSAM FIR
Abies balsamea (L.) Mill.
Pine Family

The fir tree is used as a Christmas tree because of its aromatic scent and the fact that the needles remain long after it is cut. This spire-like tree — which may attain a height of 60 feet — grows in cool woods and on higher ground.

The needles vary in length from ½ to 1¼ inches (1-3.2 cm) and have two silvery-white lines on the underside. Needles on younger trees may be *notched at the tips*. Branchlets of younger trees are flatter and have two-ranked needles, while those on older trees are usually stiffer and more rounded. Branches on younger trees are arranged in regular whorls and form a very symmetrical tree.

Cones develop in June and are dark purple until they reach maturity in August and September. They are from 1½ to 3½ inches (3-8.5 cm) long and *always grow upright* on the branchlets. The seed scales drop off soon after maturity, leaving only the central column standing.

The bark of young trees is smooth and pale gray, but that of older trees has pitch-filled blisters. The wood is light and soft and is used for pulpwood.

1. underside of twig tip
2. winter twig showing cone after disintegrating
3. upright cone on "full" branches of older trees
4. "flat" branches of younger trees showing 2-ranked foliage
5. underside of needle showing silvery bands

EASTERN HEMLOCK
Tsuga canadensis (L.) Carr.
Pine Family

enlarged winter cone

enlarged needle

Hemlock is an evergreen which attains its height of 60 to 70 feet when it grows in cool, moist sites. It likes rocky ridges and ravines. The flat terminal shoots are pendulous, and bend and sway gracefully away from prevailing winds.

The flat needles have fine teeth at the edges which may be seen with a hand lens. The needles have blunt tips, and usually several needles occur *upside down along the branchlet.* The top of the needles is a lustrus, dark, yellow-green, but the underside is whitish or silvery. The needles are much shorter than those on fir and most spruce. Each needle has a short distinct stalk, but the stalks become progressively shorter towards the tip of the stem.

The cones are about ¾ of an inch long and hang from the tip of the tiny branchlets. They are light brown, and the scales are not shiny. Cones mature in the fall and usually remain on the tree until the next spring.

The bark is divided into narrow, rounded ridges which are covered with thick scales. It varies in color from gray to cinnamon red. The twigs are very fine and limber, and have no pitch on them. When the needles are removed, the twig will be very rough — not smooth as on the fir tree.

The wood is coarse and strong — usually difficult to work with as it is apt to twist. It is used for framing buildings, sheathing, roof boards, pulpwood, and timbers.

3

CAT or WHITE SPRUCE
Picea glauca (Moench) Voss
Pine Family

cone
scale

White Spruce is abundant in the northeast, but is not as common as Red Spruce. The tree is conical in shape and is commonly from 60 to 90 feet tall when mature. The leaves have a disagreeable odor when bruised, giving rise to the alternate name of Cat or Skunk Spruce. White Spruce grows along the shores of streams and lakes, and in old pastures or cleared land where it gets the sun it needs.

The branches are stout and rigid, and the tips usually curve upward. The needle-like leaves on the lower sides are curved upward in such a way as to make one think that all needles are *on the upper side of the branchlet.* The needles are pale blue-green when young, but later become dark blue-green. The young twigs are hairless.

The slender cylindrical cones are longer (5 cm.) and thinner than those cones on the Red Spruce. They *always hang downward.* The thin, flexible scales are entire — not jagged as on the Black Spruce.

The bark on older trees is ash brown with thin, light grey scales. The wood is fairly light soft, and quite strong. It is used for pulpwood, boxes, paddles, oars, and lumber.

4

RED SPRUCE
Picea rubens Sarg.
Pine Family

Red Spruce is similar to White and Black Spruce, but can be distinguished by certain characteristics. It is different from Black Spruce because of the larger cones which fall during the first winter, while those on the Black Spruce persist. The cones on Red Spruce are more rounded than the cylindrical cones of the White Spruce, and the scales are stiff, whereas those of White Spruce cones are flexible. Also, the twigs are hairy on Red Spruce, but not on White Spruce.

The four-sided shiny, dark green needles have a yellow tinge. They are prickly to touch, are crowded on the twig, and point outward in all directions on the twig. Each needle is on a dark *brown raised projection* of the twig.

The cone (3-4 cm.) is reddish brown and shiny when mature and *hangs downward* from the branchlet. Each cone is on a short stalk, and the cone scales are rounded, not toothed like those on the Black Spruce.

The think, rough bark of mature trees has thin, close, reddish-brown scales. The wood is nonporous, light, soft, and not strong. It is primarily used for pulpwood and lumber, but is also valuable as sounding boards for musical instruments. Spruce gum is also obtained from this tree.

Red Spruce is common on mountain slopes and well-drained uplands, but is also found on the margins of swamps and streams.

cone scale

BLACK or BOG SPRUCE
Picea mariana (Mill.) BSP
Pine Family

Black Spruce is an evergreen tree, usually ten to thirty feet high in the north, but reaching a height of seventy or more feet farther south. The branches are short and have a tendency to curve upwards at the tips. The lower branches often touch the ground and take root. Black Spruce is most commonly found along streams, on borders of swamps, or in sphagnum bogs where trees more than fifty years old may be only six or eight feet tall. On some trees, a small parasitic plant — Dwarf Mistletoe — may be found (See page 94). This plant will, in time, kill the Black Spruce.

The flexible needles have blunt tips and are soft to the touch. They are from ½ to ¾ inch (6-10 mm.) long, are four-sided, and have a whitish bloom on them. The short, blue-green needles tend to curve downward towards the twig.

The egg-shaped cones are ½ to 1½ inch (2-3 cm.) long and are nearly spherical when open. They are a dull, dark brown in color. The cone scales are stiff and are *toothed on the outer edge*. Cones may stay on the trees for several years.

The dark reddish or grayish brown bark has thin scales on it. The twigs are light yellow-brown with brown glandular hairs. The reddish-tinged wood is soft, light, and not too strong. It is used for pulpwood, lumber, and piling. Spruce beer is made from the new twigs, and spruce gum is collected in winter from holes made in the trunk the previous spring.

NORWAY SPRUCE
Picea abies (L.) Karst.
Pine Family

Norway Spruce is a large spruce usually 50-80 feet in height but occasionally grows to 125 feet. It has a straight, slightly tapering, continuous trunk. On mature trees, the trunk may be free of branches for a considerable distance from the ground. Norway Spruce can be distinguished from other spruce by its *large cones and long, sweeping branches*. It prefers rather moist, rich soil and will not endure in dry, sterile soil.

The stiff, four-sided, sharp-pointed needles may be from ½ to 1 inch long. They usually point towards the tip of the twig. The needles have no real leaf stalk, but are resting on projections of the bark. The needles may be bluish green or a deep olive green.

The fruit is a large, cylindrical cone 4-7 inches (1-1.5 dm.) long which matures at the end of the first season and falls soon after maturity. The cone scales are rather broad, reddish-brown, and have finely-toothed tips. Cones usually hang downward.

Bark on old trunks is roughened with thick, reddish-brown scales. Bark on younger trees has thinner and closer scales. The twigs are *slender and usually hairless* and hang down. Remove the needles and you will see the projecting leaf bases and the tiny winter buds.

The medium-hard wood is strong, not durable in contact with soil, and close-grained. It is largely used for paper pulp, construction, and interior finish. It is not native to New England, but has been planted as an ornamental tree and has survived. It has become established in some places in Connecticut.

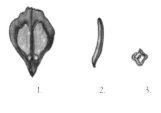

1.   2.   3.

1. a cone scale with 2-winged seeds
2. a needle
3. cross section of a needle (enlarged)

cone scale showing winged seeds

BLUE SPRUCE
Picea pungens Engelm.
Pine Family

Blue Spruce is a native of the Rocky Mountain area, but it has been frequently planted in New England as a decorative tree. It is a conical, symmetrical tree with horizontal, stout branches in whorls. This is a slow-growing tree, but is the best spruce to plant on dry lawns.

The foliage varies on different varieties of Blue Spruce, but it is a very beautiful silver-blue to blue-green. The needles are about an inch long, are stiff and sharp-pointed, and stick out at right angles to the twigs. On some varieties, the needles curve so that the tips point towards the twig.

The light brown, oblong cones are from 2½ to 4 inches long and have thin, flexible, notched scales.

AMERICAN LARCH, TAMARACK, or HACKMATACK
Larix laricina (DuRoi) K. Koch
Pine Family

American Larch is a cone-bearing tree which is *not evergreen*. It is a conical tree usually from forty to sixty feet tall with stiff, horizontal branches and lacy-looking foliage which turns ocher yellow in the fall and drops off.

The flat, needle-like leaves are slightly three-angled, blue-green in color, and are from ¾ to one inch (1-2.5 cm.) in length. They are clustered together with eight or more on each short lateral shoot, or are born singly on the terminal shoots. Small flowers form in April and May when new leaves come out.

Small ovoid cones ½ to ¾ inch (1.2-2 cm.) long — usually have less than twenty scales. These scales are usually longer than they are wide, and the greatest width is at the middle of the scale. The light, chestnut-brown cones remain on the tree all winter after the needles and seeds have fallen.

The slender, gratefully-sweeping twigs have many seams or grooves on them. The older bark has ruddy-brown or gray scales. The winter buds are reddish.

American Larch grows best in moist to boggy soils of lower lands, but also thrives on some well-drained hillsides. It makes a striking ornamental tree when not planted in dry places. The wood is hard, coarse-grained and very durable. It is used for railroad ties, telephone poles, and fence posts.

enlarged cone scale showing seeds

EUROPEAN LARCH
Larix decidua Mill.
Pine Family

European Larch is common in cultivation and has become established in the northeast. It is very similar to American Larch, but the twigs are stouter and yellower. The needles are longer (2.5-3 cm.) and the cones are a different shape. Cones on this larch are *cylindrical* and are longer (2-3.5 cm.) and larger than those on the American Larch. The flattened needles are soft, bright green and are keeled on the underside. The bark is grayish brown.

9

WHITE PINE
Pinus strobus L.
Pine Family

The abundance and value of White Pine in Maine has resulted in the name Pine Tree State and the pine cone and tassel being designated as the floral emblem of Maine. It is northern New England's most valuable tree. During colonial times, pines which were twenty-four inches or more in diameter and within three miles of water were called King's Pine and were reserved for use in the Royal Navy.

A young pine is symmetrical and conical in shape, but older trees have broad, horizontal branches and irregular-shaped tops. The trunk tapers gradually and trees often grow to be taller than one hundred feet.

The leaves are in *clusters of five* and are from three to five inches long are are soft and flexible. The papery sheath at the base of the needle cluster usually falls away. The needles are bluish green, but whitish on one side. The needles turn brownish and fall at the end of the second season.

The nodding, curved cones are thin and cylindrical, have a long stalk, and are from 4-8 inches (.6-2.5 dm.) long. It takes two years for a cone to mature and drop its seeds.

The bark of young trees is smooth and thin, but on older trees it is dark and rough, with long ridges. The wood is light in color, durable — except when in contact with the ground — and used for lumber, cabinet making, doors, interior and exterior trim, and pulpwood. Even the sawdust is used for wood flour for linoleum and wallboard. White Pine grows in many habitats, but develops best on fertile, well drained sandy soils.

RED or NORWAY PINE
Pinus resinosa Ait.
Pine Family

Red Pine is a handsome, dark green evergreen tree with a tall, straight trunk. It may reach the height of one hundred or more feet as it does in the famous "Cathedral Pines" near Eustis, Maine. The tree is *not from Norway*, but the name refers to its original discovery near Norway, Maine.

The long, flexible needles are from four to six inches (7-17cm.) in length and are in *clusters of two* in dark brown sheaths.

The cones are egg shaped, about two inches (5 cm.) long, and are borne on short stalks at right angles to the branch. Cones mature in the fall of the second season and usually remain on the branches until the following summer.

Red Pine cones are "hollow-based" due to the manner in which they are shed, leaving some basal scales on the branch. This is opposed to the "solid-based" cones of Austrian Pine which retain all of their scales when the cones are shed. Red Pine cones also lack the sharp prickles present on Austrian Pine.

The bark has flat ridges and shallow grooves on it. The coarse twigs are smooth and tan-red.

Red Pine usually grows in groves scattered throughout forests of other species. It grows best in sunny areas on dry, rocky ridges or where the soil is light and sandy. The wood is strong, hard, and light colored. It is used for construction work, and as piles, masts, and spars.

cone reduced ¾

11

AUSTRIAN PINE
Pinus nigra Arnold v. *austriaca* (Hoess.)
   Aschers. & Graebn.
Pine Family

Austrian Pine is a large pine from Europe, and when found growing in New England, it has generally been planted. It has spreading branches which form a pyramidal shape — though in old age, the tree may be rather flat-topped. It is very similar to Red Pine. The needles are in clusters of two and are 3 and 6 inches long. It can be differentiated from Red Pine because the needles do not break in two when bent, while those of the Red Pine will snap in two when bent double. The cones are attached directly to the twigs. The larger cones fall intact with the seeds remaining inside. The cone *scales have a short prickle* on the exposed surface. This surface is lighter in color than the rest of the cone. The branchlets are usually light brown. The light brown buds are resinous.

SCOTCH PINE
Pinus Sylvestris L.
Pine Family

Scotch Pine is not native to America, but has been widely planted as an ornamental and was formerly used for reforestation purposes. It is a small, often crooked tree, usually with branches which bend low and very near to the ground. Though it is a fast growing tree, it often does not develop a straight trunk. It grows in just about any soil in which it is planted, but it prefers deep, well-drained sandy loam in sunny areas.

The needles are in *clusters of two*, but are *much shorter* (2 to 3 inches) than those of the Red Pine which are also in clusters of two. The slightly twisted needles are a dull bluish-green and are very stiff. The stout twigs are brittle and yellow-gray. They are smooth, but are not glossy. The buds for the next year's needles are brown and have blunt-pointed tips.

The small cones are from 1 to 2½ inches long and have a very short stalk. They are solitary or in pairs and usually *point backwards*. The cone scales are tipped with conspicuous angular knobs. Cones are usually numerous, even on comparatively young trees.

The bark of the trunk is scaly and peels off in flakes from the ridges which are separated by long narrow, shallow grooves. A distinguishing characteristic is the conspicuous orange-brown coloration of the bark in the crown section of older trees. The bark on the lower trunk is grayish brown while the inner bark is reddish brown.

The wood is non-porous, resinous, and light reddish-brown with light yellowish or reddish sapwood. It is used for general construction, lumber, poles, and fuel.

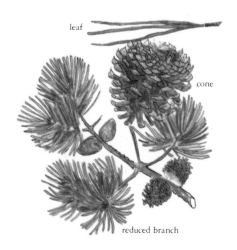

leaf

cone

reduced branch

PITCH PINE
Pinus rigida Mill.
Pine Family

Pitch Pine may reach heights up to 75 feet, but it is usually a smaller, chunky tree which grows on windswept lands where few other trees would survive. It is found on off-shore islands, sandy barrens, and on rocky ledges along the coast. It is extremely fire resistant and will sometimes be the only tree to remain alive after a forest fire.

The rigid, needle-like leaves are flattened and are usually curving. They are from 2-5 inches (3.5-14 cm.) long and come in a *bundle of three*. The needles are usually in tufts at the tips of the branches and are olive-green in color.

The stalkless, squat cones are from 1-3 inches (3-7 cm.) long and are almost as broad as they are long. Cones frequently appear in small clusters. The cone scales are terminated by a sharp prickle. After the cones open and shed their seeds, they may remain on the tree for several seasons.

The thick very rough bark is deeply furrowed and a dark reddish-brown. Clusters of needles sometimes grow right out of the bark. A sticky pitch oozes out of the buds and branches when they are bruised or disturbed. The twigs are coarse, scaly, and gray-brown.

The wood is light, soft, not strong, brittle, but it is durable. It is used mostly for posts, pulpwood, and charcoal, but was formerly tapped for turpentine and resin. It is rarely used for lumber.

JACK or GRAY PINE
Pinus banksiana Lamb.
Pine Family

Jack Pine is a scrubby, small tree usually 15-50 feet in height and often distorted or ragged in appearance. It grows in poor, dry, barren, or sandy soils and on ledges near the coast. *No other pine in our area has such short needles.*

The needles are 1-1½ inches (2-4 cm.) long, stiff, and generally curved or twisted at the base. The needles are a bright, warm, yellow-green at first but become dark green. They grow in *clusters of two* which diverge at a wide angle.

The cones take two years to mature. They usually have a bulge on one side or *curve towards the tip of the branch*. Cones are 1½-2 inches (3-5 cm.) long and the scales may have a short, weak prickle on them (this drops off as the cone ages). The mature cones may remain closed for several years and stay on the branch for as many as 10 years. Fires help the cones to open and spread their seeds.

The shaggy bark is dark, ruddy brown, but grays with age. It has irregular rounded ridges. The spreading branches are long and flexible, and often are tinged with redness.

The wood is heavy, moderately soft, not strong and is suitable for pulp, construction, box boards, and posts. It is not common enough in our area to be of commercial importance, though it may be harvested in certain localities. It makes a quick, hot fire.

MUGO or SWISS MOUNTAIN PINE
Pinus mugo Turra
Pine Family

Mugo Pine is native to the mountains of Europe but has been planted in New England. It survives, but rarely — if ever — escapes or becomes naturalized. It is usually a low, spreading or prostrate shrub, but if allowed to grow without pruning, may reach heights of 12-15 feet in New England. The branches are brown and the bright green needle-like leaves are crowded on the branchlets. The stout needles are in groups of two. Cones may be dark brown or tawny yellow and are usually quite shiny. Cones are one inch or less in length and are nearly round when fully open. This species is variable and there are several varieties listed in horticultural manuals. Mugo Pine is much used in foundation plantings because it withstands pruning and restraining well.

enlarged twig tip showing cone

NORTHERN WHITE CEDAR or ARBOR-VITAE

Thuja occidentalis L.
Pine Family

This is a medium-sized evergreen tree with a very dense, conical crown. The tapering trunk is furrowed, buttressed, and often divided or twisted. It rarely reaches a height more than fifty feet. It is more common in northern New England where it usually grows in low, swampy areas, but it does occasionally occur on hillsides farther south. The value of this tree is chiefly for ornamental purposes where it is used for wind breaks, hedges, and accent shrubbery around buildings.

The scale-like leaves are closely overlapping and the shiny, yellow-green foliage is arranged in flat fan-like clusters which are very aromatic when crushed. There are two types of alternating pairs of leaves. Those on the side of the twig have a raised keel, but those on the face of the twigs are flat.

The oblong cone, which only has from six to twelve scales, is reddish brown. It is rarely longer than ½ inch, and it matures in one season.

The bark is grayish to reddish brown and separates into long, narrow, thin strips which remain hanging on the trunk.

enlarged branch

SOUTHERN WHITE CEDAR or CYPRESS
Chamaecyparis thyoides (L.) BSP.
Pine Family

This strong-scented evergreen usually grows in swamps and bogs and is more common in southern New England. It reaches heights to 60 feet. The yellow-green leaves are small, scale-like, and have a small gland on the back. They are arranged in four rows and closely overlap each other. The needles and twigs are similar to those on *Arbor-vitae* but are smaller.

Insignificant flowers are in small, terminal, catkins — male and female on different branches. The small cones are about ¼ inch (6-9 mm.) long and are seated directly on the twig. Each cone has about three pairs of scales. The bark is brown and is divided into ridges. The wood is pale brown, soft, light, and weak, but it is exceedingly durable when in contact with the soil. It would be suitable for rails and fence posts, but it is not common enough to be extensively harvested.

COMMON or GROUND JUNIPER
Juniperus communis v. *depressa* Pursh
Pine Family

Juniper often occurs as a shrub in circular patches. It grows in poor soil of old pastures or on ledges. The branches radiate from the center and curve upwards. Juniper likes the sun and will disappear as pastures are claimed by the woods. Juniper is usually from one to three feet tall.

The needle-like leaves are 8-18 mm. long and are arranged in whorls of three which are at right angles to the stem. The *top surface i.*

enlargement showing whorl of 3 leaves

18

concave and has a broad white stripe. The bottom surface is convex and is green. The needles are sharp-pointed and are crowded on the branchlets, thus making the branches very prickly to touch or pick.

The fruit is hard and berry-like with a three-part marking on the tip. The berry-like cone is from ¼ to ⅜ inch (6-10 mm.) long and is somewhat three-sided. It is pale and waxy when young, but becomes dark blue or bluish black with a bloom when it matures. Berry-like cones are used for medicinal purposes and for the flavoring in gin.

The thin bark is reddish-brown and will peel into papery strips.

CREEPING JUNIPER or SAVIN
Juniperus horizontalis Moench
Pine Family

Creeping Juniper is a low, creeping or trailing shrub with scale-like leaves pressed close to the stem. It is found on margins of swamps, on rocky headlands near the coast, or on inland ledges. It is rare in southern New Hampshire and southern Vermont, but more common in southern Maine and along the coast.

The dark green leaves are closely-overlapping scales which usually grow opposite each other. They are similar to those on Atlantic White Cedar, but the branches on this shrub *are not flattened*. The fruit is a lobed, berry-like cone similar to that of Red Cedar. It is about the size of a pea (6-10 mm. in diameter) and is on *a short, recurved stalk or peduncle*. The berry-like cone contains 3-5 seeds and has scaly bracts below it.

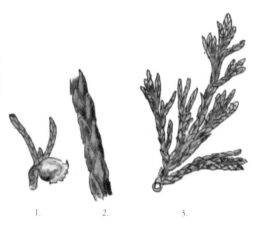

1.
2.
3.

1. fruiting branch
2. enlarged mature foliage
3. tip of a branch

RED CEDAR or SAVIN
Juniperus virginiana L.
Pine Family

Red Cedar is a small evergreen tree usually less than twenty feet tall. It is our darkest evergreen, and has a close, spire-like shape; the trunk is often ridged or buttressed at the base. It grows in dry sterile soils of old fields and hillsides or in peaty swamps.

Most red cedar trees have two kinds of foliage. The scale-like leaves of older growth or mature trees are in overlapping pairs which are pressed close to the branchlet, forming a four-sided twig. The leaves of the younger growth are needle- or awl-shaped and a little brighter in color. These needle-like leaves are mostly opposite and have three sides.

The hard fruit is whitish to slate blue or purple and is somewhat globular in shape. These berry-like cones are about ¼ inch (5-6 mm.) in diameter and have sweet flesh which is resinous. These fruits are eaten by birds.

The ruddy-brown, dry bark is shreddy, but not ridged. The bark will separate into long, narrow strips which are perpendicularly or spirally seamed. The wood is soft, light, fragrant, and durable. It is used for posts, sills, railroad ties, lead pencils and the interior finish of buildings — especially for closets where it provides protection from the house moth.

mature foliage

new growth

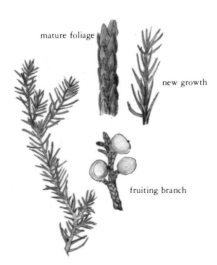

fruiting branch

COMMON GREENBRIER or HORSEBRIER

Smilax rotundifolia L.
Lily Family

Greenbrier is a tough, woody, curving vine up to 6 feet in length. The stems and branches bear *stout, flattened prickles.* It is not common in northern New England, but is an obnoxious pest in southern New England. It grows along banks of streams, at edges of swamps, and in woods and thickets. The vine climbs by means of tendrils.

The leaves are broad with a heart-shaped or rounded base. They are up to 4 inches (4.5-10 cm.) long, are tough, and are shiny on both surfaces. They have lengthwise nerves plus net-like veins.

The insignificant flowers are in clusters on stalks which rise from the axils of the leaves. The male and female flowers are on separate plants. The blue-black berry has a bloom and two seeds inside. It usually ripens in July.

BRISTLY GREENBRIER

Smilax tamnoides var. *hispida* Gray
Lily Family

This greenbrier is similar to the Common Greenbrier but has many prickles of unequal length — especially at the base of the stout stalk. The leaves are thinner and are oval-pointed and not heart shaped. The thorns are often blackish. The greenish flowers are in an umbel. The fruit is a blue-black, bitter berry with one or two seeds inside. This greenbrier grows in rich thickets, woods, and along river bottoms.

WILLOWS

There are many species of willows in New England — probably sixty or more — including both trees and shrubs. All willows have similar characteristics, but it is too difficult for anyone but a trained botanist to accurately identify many of them. For this reason, only a brief description of twenty-seven willows will be included in this book. Identifying characteristics of each will be pointed out.

Characteristics common to most willows are:

Leaves: There are alternate (except on one shrub), narrow, and pointed on most willows. The leaf stalks are either short or lacking entirely on some species.

Stipules: These are small, paired, leaf-like appendages at the base of the leaf stalk. These are present on many species — but fall off on others — and are important for correct identification.

Buds: The winter buds are covered with a single, cap-like scale with silky, gray hairs beneath that scale.

Flowers: The flowers occur early in the spring and are in catkins which are crowded with tiny beaked flowers. Male and female flowers are in separate catkins — usually on separate plants.

Fruits: The fruits are small capsules which have two valves. These are filled with seeds which have silky hairs attached to them.

The willows in this book will be separated into the following groups, and within the groups they will be listed according to *Gray's Manual of Botany*.

I. Trees
  1. *Salix nigra* Marsh.   Black Willow
  2. *Salix fragilis* L.   Crack Willow
  3. *Salix babylonica* L. Weeping Willow
  4. *Salix alba* L.   White Willow

II. Alpine Willows
  1. *Salix herbacea* L.   Dwarf Willow
  2. *Salix uva-ursi* Pursh Bearberry Willow
  3. *Salix arctophila* Cockerell
            Dwarf or Katahdin Willow
  4. *Salix argyrocarpa* Anderss.
                Silver Willow
  5. *Salix planifolia* Pursh
            Tea-Leaved Willow

III. Uncommon or Northern Shrubby Willows
  10. *Salix amygdaloides* Anderss.
            Peach-Leaved Willow
  11. *Salix interior* Rowlee
            Sand-Bar Willow
  12. *Salix glaucophylloides* Fern. Willow
  13. *Salix coactilis* Fern. Felted Willow
  14. *Salix candida* Flugge Hoary Willow
  15. *Salix pellita* Anderss. Woolly Willow

IV. Common Shrubby Willows
  16. *Salix pentandra* L. Bay-Leaved Willow
  17. *Salix lucida* Muhl.   Shiny Willow
  18. *Salix pyrifolia* Anderss.
            Balsam Willow
  19. *Salix cordata* Michx.
          Heart-Leaved Willow
  20. *Salix rigida* Muhl.
          Heart-Leaved Willow
  21. *Salix bebbiana* Sarg. Beaked Willow
  22. *Salix pedicellaris* Pursh Bog Willow
  23. *Salix discolor* Muhl.
          Large Pussy Willow
  24. *Salix humilis* Marsh.
        Dwarf Gray Pussy Willow
  25. *Salix gracilis* Anderss. Slender Willow
  26. *Salix sericea* Marsh. Silky Willow
  27. *Salix purpurea* L.
       Basket or Purple Willow

BLACK WILLOW
Salix nigra Marsh.
Willow Family

1. female catkins
2. enlarged fruit
3. enlarged stipules

Black Willow may be a shrub, but when fully developed is a tree up to 60 feet or more high with several trunks and an irregular crown. It grows on banks of streams, shores, and in rich low lands.

The leaves are from 3-6 inches (.5-1.5 dm.) long and are very narrow. The margins have fine teeth and the blade sometimes *tapers to a curved point. Both sides of the leaf are deep olive green.* The midrib may be slightly hairy and the leaf stalk and the stipules around it are hairy. The male flowers are in yellowish catkins, the stamen tips reddish. The female flowers are in whitish catkins. The fruit is a conical capsule 3-5 mm. long.

The bark of larger trees is a flaky dark brown to black and it is heavily ridged. Branchlets are brittle at the base, but tough and flexible nearer the tips. The twigs of the current year are reddish to gray brown.

The wood is soft, light, and weak and is used for baskets, packing material, boxes, and charcoal.

CRACK WILLOW
Salix fragilis L.
Willow Family

This willow is a European tree up to 100 feet in height which has been planted in New England and has spread from cultivation to roadsides and borders of woods. It resembles *Salix alba* (p. 26) but the young branchlets are *very fragile or brittle at the base.* They will easily break off with a swipe of the hand. The slender, pointed leaves are green on both sides and are 4-6 inches (1-1.5 dm.) long. The underside may be lighter in color, but it *is not hairy.* The margins have uniformly small teeth. Stipules are present at the base of the leaf stalk. The bark is thick and rough, but the branches are smooth and shiny.

Salix fragilis x alba is a hybrid willow which was long ago introduced in this country as a tree which was resistant to blight. It has become our most common tree willow and is the one most often misidentified. It grows along streams and rivers near habitation. People have identified this tree as Crack Willow, but actually it is a cross between Crack Willow and White Willow.

WEEPING WILLOW
Salix babylonica L.
Willow Family

Though the true Weeping Willow has the Latin name given above, most Weeping Willows growing in yards, parks and along streets are actually a horticultural variety of trees known as *Salix niobe.* They are similar, but the *niobe* is more resistant to blight than the native *babylonica.*

Weeping Willow is a tree with extraordinary, pendulous branchlets with many narrow leaves, up to 5 inches (2-12 cm.) in length. The stout trunk may be five or six feet in diameter on a Weeping Willow when it reaches its maximum height of seventy feet. It grows in wet places, and is easily propagated by sticking branches in wet ground until they take root. Weeping Willow is a fast growing tree, chiefly used as an ornamental. The greenish-yellow catkins are not very spectacular, and might even be mistaken for new foliage. These catkins appear on the hanging branches, near the ends, but not at the very tips.

enlarged leaf margin

WHITE WILLOW
Salix alba L.
Willow Family

White Willow was widely planted in the past and has escaped and naturalized itself in moist soils. It is a large tree up to 90 feet in height.

The slender, lance-shaped leaves have grayish, silky hairs on both sides (these may be seen with a hand lens). The leaves are not as large or as wide as those on *S. fragilis*, which it resembles. The leaves are olive-green on the top and are grayish underneath. There are several varieties of this willow, and each differs slightly from the one shown. Some varieties are hairy on the underside while others are not. The midribs are paler in color than the leaf itself. The branches are silky and pendulous. They are flexible and not brittle at the base. The twigs are yellow-tan to gray-brown.

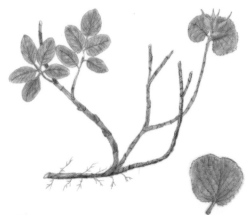

DWARF WILLOW
Salix herbacea L.
Willow Family

Dwarf Willow is a sub-alpine willow which is found on Mt. Katahdin in Maine and on the White Mountains of New Hampshire. It is a very small, matted shrub only 5-8 inches tall. It grows in gravelly soil and in crevices at higher elevations. The *trunk and main branches are underground*. The plant takes root at nodes and thus forms large mats.

Usually there are from 2-6 small leaves crowded at the tips of the upright branches. These are lustrous and net-veined. The tips may be rounded or have an indentation at the center. The larger leaves are shaped like a mouse's ear.

The yellow-green, beaked fruits are in a small cluster amid the crowded leaves at the tip of the branches. Each beaked fruit has hairy seeds inside.

BEARBERRY WILLOW
Salix uva-ursi Pursh
Willow Family

Bearberry Willow is a sub-alpine shrub which grows close to the ground and is seldom more than 6-8 inches tall. It is a low, matted, widely-spreading plant which grows in dry areas at higher elevations. It grows in barren, gravelly soil, rocky ground, and on steep slopes on Mt. Katahdin and other mountains in the Presidential Range.

Many leaves are clustered together towards the tips of the branches. The small leaves are longer than broad, but the widest part is above the middle. There may be a few inconspicuous teeth on the margins. The leaves are shiny green above and pale beneath. The flower catkins blossom in June and are very conspicuous. Many brown branches arise from a deep central root. The bark is very rough and dark.

DWARF or KATAHDIN WILLOW
Salix arctophila Cockerell
Willow Family

This willow is very rare — probably the rarest willow in New England. It has only been found on Mt. Katahdin in Maine. It is a low, trailing shrub found in barrens, meadows or near open granite slopes of alpine areas.

The leaves are round-oval and are clustered at the tips of the branches. The rather leathery leaves are dark green and lustrous above and have red leaf stalks. The tips may be rounded or have a single point at the tip. There are no stipules at the leaf axils.

The stout twigs trail on the ground. The bark is dark brown — almost black. The buds are very dark brown and hairy. Close inspection with a hand lens shows that the twigs are hairy, especially at the leaf nodes.

SILVER WILLOW
Salix argyrocarpa Anderss.
Willow Family

This willow is a small *rose-colored shrub* which grows in alpine meadows or on wet rocks at higher elevations. It is usually from 6 inches to 2 feet tall. It is very rare, but has been found on Mt. Katahdin.

The earliest leaves are ovate with the widest part being above the middle of the leaf, but later leaves are very narrow and taper at both ends. The leaves are bright green on the upper surface, and have a distinct orange mid-rib and silvery-silky, glistening, minute hairs on the underside. The edges of the leaf are rolled under and there are very tiny stipules at the leaf axils. The conical fruit capsule also has silvery, glistening hairs. The reddish twigs are very "nubby" with projections where the old leaf stalks were attached.

TEA-LEAVED WILLOW
Salix planifolia Pursh
Willow Family

Tea-Leaved Willow is a rare, much-branched shrub rarely as tall as three feet. It grows in moist areas on high mountains of New England and Canada, and has been found on Mt. Katahdin in Maine.

This willow is similar to Silver Willow and grows in the same habitats, but the leaves on this willow are shiny and dark or dull green on both sides. The underside may be paler in color, but there *are no hairs*. The elliptical leaves are pointed at the tip and the base. Usually the margins are untoothed, but there may be a few uneven, minute teeth. There are a few rudimentary leaves at the base, but the larger leaves are at the tips of the branches. The branchlets are purplish or dark colored.

male flower   female capsule

PEACH-LEAVED WILLOW
Salix amygdaloides Anderss.
Willow Family

Peach-Leaved Willow is a coarse shrub or small tree up to 40-50 feet in height. It grows along shores, in low woods and in swamps.

The alternate leaves are broadly lance-shaped and have a long point and *fine toothed margins*. The underside of the leaf is whitish or grayish. The stipules are very small and usually vanish by late spring. Young leaves are hairy and the midrib is yellow or orange.

Flowers are in catkins which appear with the leaves. The male flowers have five stamens and are in catkins 1-2 inches long. The female flower produces long capsules with a "V" at the top.

These fruits are in loose and spreading catkins 2½-4 inches long.

The bark is reddish-brown to black and is often scaly or ridged and furrowed. The twigs are usually drooping and yellowish or yellow-brown in color.

SANDBAR WILLOW
Salix interior Rowlee
Willow Family

Sandbar Willow is usually a much-branched shrub which forms dense thickets along edges of rivers, but it occasionally grows to the size of a small tree of twenty feet or so. It grows in gravel and sands — especially along rivers. A large number grow along the Connecticut River.

The alternate leaves are narrow, 2-6 inches long, and have tiny, *wide-spaced marginal teeth* which may be almost obscure on some leaves. The tip is pointed, the leaf base is tapering, and the leaf stalk is very short. The leaf may be hairless or rather silky — especially on young foliage. The leaf is yellow green on the top and a paler green underneath. The *mid rib is yellowish* and the stipules are very small — or are lacking entirely.

The bark is dark, reddish-brown and is scaly. The branches are short, slender, orange to purplish-red and are erect. The twigs are hairless and gray.

WILLOW
Salix glaucophylloides Fern.
Willow Family

This willow is very uncommon in New England, but does occur on gravelly riverbanks and shores and in rich thickets in the limy areas of northern Maine. It is a shrub or small tree up to 15 feet in height.

The lustrous-green leaves resemble those on Bog Willow, but are longer and narrower — 1 to 3 inches (3-12 cm.) long. The oblong to elliptic-oblong leaves have a short point and the base may be rounded, heart-shaped or tapering. The margins have small, obscure, gland-tipped teeth. The leaves have a rather thin texture and the underside is whitened and has a prominent, yellowish midrib. Leaves will blacken in drying.

The twigs are yellowish or greenish to a chestnut-brown. Though new twigs may be somewhat velvety, they soon become smooth and shiny. The stipules are somewhat heart-shaped and many will remain on the twigs as the leaves mature.

FELTED WILLOW

Salix coactilis Fern.
Willow Family

Felted Willow is a shrub usually from 5-12 feet tall. It grows in rich swamps and along streams. The *leaves have scalloped margins.* The horizontally divergent, unequal teeth are gland tipped. Young leaves are heavily felted with silky hairs or plush on the underside. Mature leaves are dark green above and are paler or somewhat whitish underneath. These leaves turn brown or black when dried. Mature leaves are narrow or oval-pointed with scalloped margins which taper to a rounded base. The toothed stipules will fall off as foliage matures. The slender twigs are purplish to black.

HOARY WILLOW
Salix candida Fluegge
Willow Family

Hoary Willow is a shrub up to 6 feet in height. It grows in cold bogs and thickets, occurring rarely in northern Maine, and only scattered throughout Vermont. The leaves are usually erect or nearly so, and are inclined to overlap in tufts on stout branches. The top surface of the leaves is slightly molded and dull in color. The undersurface is fuzzy with white or gray hairs. The untoothed margin is rolled under and the point is rather blunt. Stipules are present at the base of the leaf stalk.

This willow is similar to *Salix pellita* (below), but the leaves are wider. The undersurface of the leaves is more plush on this leaf than on those of *S. pellita*. The leaf tip is more pointed on *S. pellita* than on this willow.

The stout branches are brown with gray or white woolly hairs. Older branches are apt to be more reddish in color.

WOOLLY WILLOW
Salix pellita Anderss.
Willow Family

Woolly Willow is a low shrub or small tree, usually not much taller than 8 feet. It grows along stream banks, in moist, rich thickets and in swamps in northern New England. The branchlets are olive or tan and are whitened by a powder on the surface. The larger twigs are reddish-brown and are not hairy.

The long, narrow leaves are dark gray-green on the upper surface and are very hairy. The underside is a beautiful, rich, silvery-white silky velvet. The thick, firm leaves have margins which are strongly rolled under. The stipules fall off early.

BAY-LEAVED WILLOW
Salix pentandra L.
Willow Family

Bay-Leaved Willow may be a shrub or a small tree up to 25 feet. The pointed, oval leaves have margins with fine, even teeth of uniform size. The leaf is *shiny on both sides,* or may be slightly paler below. The leaf stalk has large glands on it, and new leaves may be gummy as they unfold.

This willow looks similar to *S. lucida* which follows, but the leaves are not as long-pointed as *S. lucida*. The shiny *twigs are not hairy.* The buds are slender, shiny, and yellow when first formed, but they turn blackish during the winter.

fruiting branch

enlarged winter twig

SHINING WILLOW
Salix lucida Muhl.
Willow Family

Shining Willow may be a small tree up to 25 feet in height or a shrub which grows in moist soil in low ground, on shores, and in swamps.

The alternate leaves are *shiny on both sides and have an extremely long tapering point.* The base of the leaf may be rounded or tapering, and the stipules at the leaf axils are conspicuous and glandular. There are two varieties of this willow. One has smooth leaves, but the varity *intonsa* has wine-colored hairs.

The flowers appear in catkins before the leaves unfold. Male and female flowers are on separate plants. Male flowers are orange-yellow and usually have five stamens. The fruit is a small, pointed capsule with a rounded base.

These are massed on a drooping, straw-colored or greenish catkin.

The bark is smooth, thin, bitter, and brown to reddish-brown. The twigs are shiny yellow-brown at first but later turn dark brown. The buds are smooth and oval-pointed, about ¼ inch long, and are covered by a single yellowish-brown scale.

twig with mature leaves

BALSAM WILLOW
Salix Pyrifolia Anderss.
Willow Family

The leaves and buds of the Balsam Willow *produce a strong balsam fragrance* when dried. This willow is a tall bush, usually less than 20 feet in height, which grows by water in roadside ditches, boggy woods, or low, wet thickets. It is found from the Presidential Range northward and westward in New England.

Young leaves are very thin and are nearly transparent — often tinged with purple. Mature leaves are firmer and may be short-oval with a short point or longer and more lance-shaped. The base may be somewhat heart-shaped or rounded, and the leaf has a long *slender red leaf stalk*. The leaf margins have minute, glandular teeth. The upperside of the leaf is deep olive green with the veins sunken in to give the appearance of fine-grained leather. The underside has a *silvery sheen* with prominent veins and a lighter or reddish midrib. The stipules are very minute or may be lacking entirely.

The twigs may be reddish or olive green and are very, very shiny — appearing almost as if someone had *varnished* them. The branchlets are brittle at the base, and there is no hair on the twigs.

HEART-LEAVED WILLOW
Salix cordata Michx.
Willow Family

Though this willow is called Heart-Leaved Willow, the bases of the leaves are often not as heart-shaped as the leaves on *S. rigida*. This willow may be a shrub up to 12 feet in height, or reach the size of a tree of 50 feet or more. It grows on gravelly or sandy shores, beaches, and sand dunes from Maine to Cape Cod. It has *large conspicuous, toothed stipules.*

Young leaves are sometimes hairy. Mature leaves are long and are broadly lance-shaped with a tapering point and finely- and evenly-toothed margins. Both sides of the leaves are green, but the underside may be paler in color. The leaf stalks and midribs are especially hairy. Leaves will reamain green in drying. Leaves vary greatly in size.

There are reddish, pointed buds in the axils of the leaves. Branchlets are densely covered with gray hairs.

HEART-LEAVED WILLOW
Salix rigida Muhl.
Willow Family

Heart-Leaved Willow is a shrub which seldom gets taller than 10 feet. It grows on sandy, rocky beaches and on the flooded shores of a swiftly-flowing river. It has *conspicuous wine-colored or reddish new leaves.*

The narrow leaves are long-oblong to lance-shaped and may be heart-shaped or broadly-rounded at the base. They are green and smooth on both sides, but the prominent midrib underneath and the leaf stalks have soft hairs on them. There are conspicuous toothed stipules at the axis of the leaves. Leaf margins are toothed.

New growth has vigorous, long branches with larger blades and stipules. Though older twigs are not hairy, new growth may have soft hairs on the twigs.

BEAKED WILLOW
Salix bebbiana Sarg.
Willow Family

Beaked Willow is a shrub or a small, bushy tree rarely exceeding 20 feet in height. It grows in swamps, along borders or streams, and in moist to dry thickets.

The alternate, elliptical or oval-pointed leaves are 1-3 inches (3-8 cm.) long. The tip is pointed, but the point is not long and tapering. The margin is sparingly-toothed and may even be toothless on the lower half of the leaf. New leaves are pale green but later become dull and are *usually hairy* — especially along the midrib and veins on the undersurface. The *veins are very prominent* on the underside, and appear to be sunken on the upper surface.

Flowers appear in April and May before or while the leaves are unfolding. The *bracts of the catkins are yellow*. The capsule is narrow with an oval base which tapers to a *long-beaked tip*. Many of these hairy capsules occur together in a lax, open catkin.

The bark is greenish gray, olive green, or may be tinged with red. The bark on trunks is usually thin and smooth, but may have shallow fissures. The branches are reddish-brown and the twigs are hairy at first — then become smooth, slender, and purplish to brown. Oval buds are blunt-pointed, about ¼ inch long, and are covered by a single, light-brown scale. They are reddish-pink or old rose colored and are rather small on this willow.

1. a female flower (enlarged)
2. twig with leaf scar and bud (enlarged)
3. leaf with stipules

38

BOG WILLOW

Salix pedicellaris Pursh
Willow Family

This willow grows in acid bogs and along shores. It is a loosely-branching shrub — usually not much taller than three feet. It has smooth, erect branches with *no stipules at the leaf axils.*

There are three varieties of this willow. The typical variety is shown. It has purplish, elliptical or oblong leaves with a rather rounded or slightly pointed tip. The leaves are very smooth and hairless on both sides. The margin is evenly curved with *no teeth or indentations.* The margins may be rolled under (revolute). The leaves are a shade paler underneath, but there is *no whitish bloom.* In variety *hypoglauca,* the leaves are whitened with a bloom on the underside. In variety *tenuescens,* the leaves are pointed at each end and are very whitened beneath. The bog willow has dark brown stems, and the midveins are orange-brown.

enlarged female capsule

male catkin

LARGE PUSSY WILLOW
Salix discolor Muhl.
Willow Family

Almost everyone knows the pussy willow in early spring, but later on, one may need to know certain characteristics in order to identify it from other willows.

The "pussies" form before the leaves. These are the developing buds of the flowering catkins. The leaves which come later are smooth, bright green above and are whitish underneath. Though they are quite variable, on the average the leaves of this willow are much broader than the slender leaves on other willows. They may be from 1½ to 4 inches (3-10 cm.) in length. The margins are irregularly-toothed — especially near the middle. They are elliptical or may be slightly wider beyond the middle. The stipules are toothed.

This willow looks similar to *S. humulis*, but the underside of the leaf is either hairless or *has both white and gray hairs*, while *S. humulis* has only gray hairs.

DWARF GRAY WILLOW or SMALL PUSSY WILLOW
Salix humulis Marsh.
Willow Family

This willow is a shrub 7-8 feet tall which grows on dry land and has wand-like flowering branches. It flowers in the early spring and resembles the more common Pussy Willow. It looks like *S. discolor*, but has *only gray hairs* on the underside, while Pussy Willows have both white and gray hairs on the leaves. If this willow grows in the shade, there will be no hairs on it. The leaves are broadest near or above the middle and the margin is rolled under. There are usually no teeth, but some leaves may have a few obscure marginal teeth. The upper surface of the leaves is not wrinkled and is chalky or gray-green in color. The midrib is yellowish. The twig is blotched or rather sooty, and has hairs on it.

SLENDER WILLOW
Salix gracilis Anderss.
Willow Family

Slender Willow is a many-stemmed shrub — usually not taller than 10 feet — which grows in wet meadows or swales. It has slender, erect branches which are tough and very flexible. The leaves are overlapping, and the stipules are present at the base of the leaf stalk.

The long slender leaves have small uniform teeth on the margins. Young leaves may be silvery as they expand, but mature leaves have a bluish cast to them. The upper surface is olive green and rather lustrous, though not as shiny as other willows. The underside is paler in color and is typically *not hairy*, though some varieties of this willow may have some hairs on the underside of the leaf. The twigs are dark brown to purplish on some varieties, while they are green or olive-brown on others. Young leaves become dark when dried, but mature leaves retain their color when pressed.

SILKY WILLOW
Salix sericea Marsh.
Willow Family

Silky Willow is a long, straggling shrub which grows in low, wet thickets and along banks of streams. It is usually not more than 12 feet tall. The long, narrow leaves taper to a *point at both ends*. The top surface is a dark green, but the entire under surface is covered with silvery-silky hairs. The lower surface is very lustrous and will shine when sunlight hits it. The margins are uniformly fine-toothed all the way to the base. There are stipules on new sprout growth, but these soon fall off. The twigs are fine, hairy, and extremely fragile. The branchlets are purplish or brownish and have bristles at the base. Another identifying characteristic is that this willow will turn black when it is dried and pressed.

BASKET or PURPLE WILLOW
Salix purpurea L.
Willow Family

This willow was introduced from Europe for use in basket making, and has occasionally escaped to nearby lowlands — especially near the coast. It is a tall, slender shrub which is rarely over 20 feet tall. It has long, slender shoots and branches which are very supple and flexible. It is the only willow in our area which has *some of its leaves almost opposite*. The narrow leaves are wider near the tip and taper gradually to the base. The margins may be untoothed or may have a few remote teeth near the ends of the leaf. The leaves have a purplish or bluish cast to the upper surface but the underside is paler. The bark is smooth and bitter. The bark on the shoots and branches is often purplish or reddish.

AMERICAN ASPEN
Populus tremuloides Michx.
Willow Family

Quaking Aspen, Popple, Trembling Aspen, or Trembling Poplar are all names given to this tree. It is a rather small tree, usually less than forty feet in height, but occasionally up to seventy feet. The trunk gradually tapers to the top of the tree. The alternating, slender branches are scattered along the trunk.

The alternate leaves are broad and heart-shaped or nearly round in general outline. They are dull — not shiny — and have finely-toothed margins. The upper surface is a dark blue-green with lighter colored veins. The leaf stalks are long and flattened nearest the leaf but round and slender near the twig. This causes the leaves to hang down and move and flutter in the slightest breeze.

Male and female flowers appear on different trees in drooping catkins. These catkins are from 1½ to 2½ inches long at first, but may lengthen to four inches at maturity.

The bark on younger trees is gray in color with a whitish bloom and dark blotches below the branches. The bark is horizontally marked. The bark on older trees is rough, dark brown or black, and thick towards the base with perpendicular, short, furrows. The branchlets are slender and warm gray, but new twigs are smooth, tan or reddish-brown, and shiny. Winter buds are narrow and cone-like with a sharp point and six or seven reddish-brown scales.

Trembling Aspen grows on dry ground and is common in abandoned fields, cut-over areas, and burns. The wood is a pale brown or nearly white, soft, weak, and not durable. It is used for the interior finish of houses, for boxes, and as pulpwood.

BIG-TOOTHED or
LARGE-TOOTHED ASPEN,
LARGE-TOOTHED POPLAR
Populus grandidentata Michx.
Willow Family

This poplar can easily be distinguished from other poplars by the large, widely-separated teeth on the leaves and by the white cottony covering on the lower surface of new growth in the spring. This fuzz gradually wears off the leaves of older trees, but it remains on the leaves of saplings. Large-Toothed Aspen grows best in rich, moist, sandy soil. It is not a large tree — usually less than sixty feet in height.

The alternate leaves are simple and broad. They are pointed at the tip, have coarse teeth at the margins, and are usually three or four inches long. They are dark green on the top and a paler green on the underside. The veins are a lighter color and are quite noticeable. Leaf *stalks are flattened* and are tinged with yellow and red.

Flowers occur in April and May. Male and female flowers occur on different trees. They are both in long, drooping catkins which are closely packed with individual flowers.

Bark near the base of older trunks is black, very rough, hard, and thick. There are large, smooth surfaces found on flat ridges between the fissures. Smaller branches have a more pronounced yellow color. The rather stout twigs are reddish to yellowish-brown but are often covered with a pale or gray woolly or crusty coat which peels off in small flakes. Winter buds are conical and usually covered with six or seven light chestnut-brown scales.

The wood is fine in texture, light in color, and neither strong nor durable. It is a principal food for beavers and is used for pulpwood, boxes, kegs, and wooden dishes.

WHITE POPLAR or
SILVER POPLAR
Populus alba L.
Willow Family

White Poplar is a medium-sized tree which usually does not get taller than thirty-five or forty feet. It is planted as an ornamental because of the beautiful contrast between the upper and lower surfaces of the leaves.

The shiny, dark green leaves have heavy white wool on the undersides. The leaves have long leaf stalks which also are covered with white fuzz. Each leaf has from three to five toothed and pointed lobes, and the base of the leaf can be either rounded or heart-shaped. Some leaves are without lobes and are merely coarsely-toothed.

The bark is a smooth, whitish-gray but it may be rough at the base of some older trees. The young branchlets, buds, and twigs are also covered with a white cottony felt which rubs off easily.

COTTONWOOD
Populus deltoides Marsh.
Willow Family

Cottonwood is our largest *Populus*. It is usually from 50-75 feet but sometimes reaches heights well over 100 feet. The tapering trunk sometimes has no branches for a considerable distance from the ground. The crown is usually high and pyramidal in shape with the lower lateral branches horizontal to the ground, and the upper branches slanting upward.

Cottonwood prefers the rich, moist soil near banks of streams or borders of swamps and lakes. In northern New England, it is not native, but has been planted as an ornamental.

The simple, triangular leaves are alternate and have coarsely-toothed margins. They are from 3-5 inches (6-12 cm.) long, are rather thick, and are shiny green on top and a paler green underneath. The long *leafstalks are flattened*.

The flowers appear in March or April with the male and female flowers occurring on different trees. The male flowers are in densely-flowered drooping catkins 3-4 inches long. The female catkins are rather sparsely flowered and are not quite as long at first — but they lengthen in maturity.

Bark on old trunks is thick, ashy-gray, and is roughened by conspicuous furrows and ridges which usually are parallel lengthwise. The bark on younger trees is thin, smooth, and yellow-green. The round, stout twigs are ochre-yellow tinged with brown or green, and have prominent ridges below the buds, running down from the leaf scars (see insert).

The large buds are alternate, chestnut brown and covered with numerous bud scales which are resinous on the inside and smooth on the outside. The terminal buds are often five-angled and are larger than the other buds.

The wood is soft, warps easily, and is difficult to split. It is used for paper pulp, boxes, crates, and similar articles.

female catkins

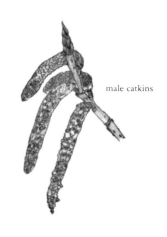

male catkins

enlarged male flower   enlarged female flower

LOMBARDY POPLAR

Populus nigra L. var. *italica* Muenchh.
Willow Family

Lombardy Poplar is a tall spire-like tree with numerous erect branches which are close to the main trunk and form a narrow column-like crown. The branches begin very close to the ground. Lombardy Poplar was frequently planted as an ornamental and has spread from the parent trees by roots· or underground shoots.

The alternate leaves have long *flattened leaf stalks* which may be tinged with red. The pointed leaf blade is broader than it is long. The leaf is usually triangular in shape, but some may be diamond-shaped. There are small teeth on the margins.

Very few trees produce seeds because most trees produce only male catkins. The trees can reproduce by sending up new shoots. The wood is rarely used, as the tree is planted chiefly for its ornamental value.

BALSAM POPLAR
Populus balsamifera L.
Willow Family

Balsam Poplar is more common in northern New England where it grows along rivers and at borders of swamps. It is a medium sized tree, usually from twenty to sixty feet in height. The trunk is straight and the branches are erect and stout — rather contorted at the ends.

The alternate, deep, dark green leaves are shiny on the top, but brownish or silvery white underneath. The veins are very noticeable on the underside, and usually there are rusty blotches. The leaf stalks on this poplar are *round*, not flattened as those on the others. The leaves are thick and firm, rather leathery in texture. They vary in length from 3-5 inches (5-12 cm.), taper at both ends, and have a pointed tip and finely-toothed margins.

The flowers are in catkins which appear early in the spring just before the leaves come out. The fruit ripens at the end of May or into June. Each seed is attached to a cottony mass and is blown about by the wind.

The bark on younger trees is smooth and light umber-brown with a ruddy tinge. Bark on older trees is dark gray with a ruddy tinge. The trunk has long seams and rough, rounded ridges. The twigs are orange or tan, usually smooth and shiny, but covered with a waxy substance which peels off. The spring buds are large, long, and pointed. They are a shiny, reddish brown, are very sticky, and have the fragrance of balsam.

The wood is light, soft, pale brown or whitish and is used for boxes, household woodenware, glue, and pulpwood.

enlarged female flower

BALM-OF-GILEAD
X. *Populus gileadensis* Rouleau
Willow Family

The Balm-of-Gilead tree is similar to the Balsam Poplar, but it has wider spreading branches which form a broader crown and a more rounded shape. It is probably an infertile hybrid of *Populus deltoides* and *Populus balsamifera*. Balm-of-Gilead is a large tree usually 50-80 feet in height but sometimes up to 100 feet. It grows along roads and streams where it has spread from cultivation. In past years, it was frequently planted in northern New England.

The rather heart-shaped leaves resemble the leaves on Balsam Poplar, but are broader and the leaf stalk and lower surface of the leaf are hairy. The leaves are dark green above and pale beneath.

Only female flowers are produced on most trees. These are in catkins about six inches (15 cm.) long. Because the tree does not produce seeds, it must be propagated by sprouts and cuttings.

The old bark is gray and ridged, but young twigs are dark brown and hairy — especially at the nodes. The resinous buds are pointed and the side buds have three visible scales. The wood is brown, soft, and weak, and is not used commercially.

SWEET GALE
Myrica Gale L.
Wax-Myrtle Family

fruit

Sweet Gale is a widely-branching shrub with thin, blunt-tipped leaves and very dark brown ascending stems. It only grows in wet places, and is common on margins of ponds, streams, and swamps. It is a spreading shrub usually not taller than four feet.

The alternate, rather dry, stiffish leaves have one main central rib. Veins are more noticeable on the underside of the leaf, which is also lighter in color. The broadest part of the leaf is at the tip and only the tip is toothed. Younger leaves may be downy on the underside, but older leaves are usually smooth. The leaves are aromatic when crushed.

Usually — but not always — the male and female flower catkins are on separate plants. The short, scaly male catkins are in terminal clusters. These catkins have large, lustrous brown bracts. The female "cones" are in the axils of the leaves or at the end of last year's wood.

The fruits are small nuts which are resin covered and look more like berries. There are two thick scales at the base of each fruit. Usually from two to six nutlets are in a cluster.

The twigs are smooth or rusty, dark brown or purplish in color, but are often spotted with yellow dots. Sometimes the twigs end with false buds. Winter buds are oval and pale in color.

BAYBERRY or WAX MYRTLE

Myrica pensylvanica Loisel.
Wax-Myrtle Family

Bayberry is a spreading, much-branched shrub with many leaves. It is abundant in sandy and sterile areas along the coast, and is occasionally found inland. It is rarely taller than six feet, and is usually about three feet tall.

The thin, rather egg-shaped leaves are one or two inches (2-5 cm.) long and only have a few teeth, or none at all. The leaves are covered with resinous dots which are visible under a hand lens. Inconspicuous flowers of two kinds develop. The female flower develops into crowded clusters of small, round, hard white "berries" which remain on the plant all winter. These are not true berries and are not edible — except by birds. The fruit was boiled by early settlers to get wax from which they made fragrant bayberry candles.

The twigs are grayish brown and are rather thick and stout. The bark of the lower part of the shrub is smooth and gray.

SWEET FERN
Comptonia peregrina (L.) Coult.
Wax-Myrtle Family

Sweet Fern is *not a fern*. It is a small aromatic shrub — up to two feet in height — which grows in sandy or sterile areas of northern New England especially on sandy banks along country roads, on blueberry barrens, or in dry, rocky pastures.

The alternate leaves are a dark olive-green. They are shiny on the top but paler underneath. At the leaf axils, there is a pair of yellow-green pointed stipules which look like green horns. The base of each "horn" covers the woody stem, but is not attached to it. The leaves are from three to six inches long and have a rolled-back edge with rounded, fern-like divisions.

The flowers are in brownish catkins, the male and female usually being on separate plants. These appear in early spring before the leaves unfold. The male catkin is drooping and nearly an inch long, while the female catkin is round.

The fruit is a small shiny nut which is enclosed in a bur-like structure. The nut has a delicate flavor when young, and may be removed from the "bur" and eaten raw.

male catkins

female catkins

bur-like fruit

53

greatly reduced leaf

BUTTERNUT or WHITE WALNUT
Juglans cinerea L.
Walnut Family

    Butternut trees are usually thirty to fifty feet tall, but occasionally grow to ninety feet in height. Heavy lower branches extend almost horizontally from the trunk. In the spring, the budding tree is greenish yellow, but in autumn the leaves turn bright yellow. Butternut grows in rich woods and on moist hillsides and especially along roads or near buildings.

    The large, alternate, very long, compound leaves may have from 7-17 leaflets, but most commonly there are eleven. The underside of the leaflets and the leaf stalks are hairy and the margins have very shallow teeth.

    Both male and female flowers develop on the same tree. The male flowers are in brown catkins which develop in May. The female flowers are in spikes — usually 6-8 together — and may occur on the same branch with the male flowers.

    The fruit may be from 1¾ to 3 inches long and is covered with a sticky, hairy husk which is yellow-green in summer, but turns brown after a frost. The shell of the nut inside has exceedingly sharp and rough ridges and is pointed at both ends. The edible nut meat is two-lobed at the base and is very sweet and oily.

    The bark is light, brownish gray. Older trees are seamed with short, flat-topped ridges while bark on younger trees is comparatively smooth. The twigs are very light brown. Newer twigs are covered with sticky hairs and are greenish and rather coarse. Older twigs become smooth and brown, and have small white spots on them. The pith inside is dark brown and is separated by hollow spaces at regular intervals (chambered). The leaf scars are three-lobed and have a pad of hairs above them.

The wood is soft and not strong. It is used for furniture, interior furnishings, and occasionally in church altars and floors.

BLACK WALNUT
Juglans nigra L.
Walnut Family

Black Walnut is a large tree which usually grows to eighty or a hundred feet in height, but may reach heights up to one hundred fifty feet. The trunk is straight, tapered, and bears a round-topped crown. It prefers rich, moist soil and requires plenty of light and very deep soil.

The alternate, compound leaves are bright yellow-green above and somewhat downy and paler below. There is fuzz on the mid rib and leaf stems. The leaf may be one or two feet long with from fifteen to twenty-three thin, toothed leaflets which are arranged in pairs. The leaflets may be lopsided at the base and have very short stalks — or none at all. The terminal leaflet is usually absent.

Both male and female flowers are on the same tree — usually on the same branch. Male flowers are in unbranched catkins while female flowers are in spikes or groups of from two to five.

The fruit is a roughly-corrugated nut which is enclosed in a smooth, green spherical husk which *does not split when ripe*. The fruits are usually in clusters of two or three; are 1½ to 2 inches in diameter; and give an iodine-like stain to the fingers. The nut meat is rather oily, but delicious.

The bark of mature trees is furrowed and dark brown to black. The pith inside is buff colored and is separated by hollow spaces at regular intervals (chambered). Twigs are

enlarged twig showing pith inside

greatly reduced leaf

covered with a brown fuzz. Terminal buds are blunt-pointed, fuzzy gray, and covered with a few hairy scales.

The wood is a rich, dark brown, very strong and durable. It is highly prized for gunstocks, furniture, and musical instruments.

BITTERNUT HICKORY or PIGNU'
Carya cordiformis (Wang.) K. Koch
Walnut Family

reduced leaf

4.

3.

1.   2.

1. section of winter branch showing buds
2. enlarged leaf scar with bundle scars
3. twig with mature fruit and leaf
4. male catkins

Bitternut Hickory is a tall tree usually from 40-80 feet in height but reaching heights up to 100 feet. It is not found in Maine, but is common in southern New England — especially in mountainous regions. It grows in moist soils in swamps or rich woodlands.

The compound leaves are from 6-10 inches long and have from 7-11 narrow, pointed leaflets. These have fine-toothed margins, a deep-yellow green color on top, and are paler and slightly hairy on the under side.

The flowers appear when the leaves are half developed. Male flowers are in greenish catkins 3-4 inches long which are arranged in groups of three. The female flowers are about ½ inch long in small clusters amidst the new growth.

The fruit is an ovoid, thin-shelled, four-ribbed nut about an inch long. This nut is enclosed in a thin yellow-scaly husk which *splits about half way at maturity*. The nut is pointed at the tip and the kernel inside is edible but becomes bitter with age.

The bark is light gray and smooth on younger trunks. On older trunks it has narrow ridges and shallow furrows. It is tight-fitting and *does not peel or flake* as bark on some of the other hickories does. The twigs are slender, smooth, and glossy and are often yellow-glandular and hairy near the tips. They may be grayish, orange-brown and even pale red but are roughened with long, pale marks called lenticels. It is the only native hickory with *yellow buds*. The sulfur yellow buds are scurfy and have ½-inch long scales which do not overlap. The leaf scars are heart-shaped and lighter in color than the twigs, and have bundle-scars arranged in three groups — usually in a single curved line.

The wood is hard, heavy, and strong — though not as strong as the other hickories. It is suitable for fuel, but not as good as other hickories.

SHAGBARK HICKORY
Carya ovata (Mill.) K. Koch
Walnut Family

Shagbark Hickory is a tall tree up to ninety feet in height. It is more common in southern New England where it grows in dry, rich woods. Farther north it is planted near roads and houses for its edible nuts.

The large compound leaves are from eight to twenty inches long with five (occasionally nine) toothed, leaflets. The three terminal leaflets are the largest. There is a minute *tuft of hair on each tooth.*

The male and female reproductive parts are in separate flowers. The male flowers are arranged in three-branched catkins which are four or five inches long. The female flowers are rusty, woolly spikes — usually from two to five together in the leaf axils.

The fruit is a nearly round nut with a hard, smooth, four-ribbed, light-brown shell. The shells are hard to crack, but the meat inside is delicious and worth the effort. The nut is enclosed in a thick, reddish-brown to black husk which splits into four parts when ripe.

Mature trees have distinctive shaggy bark composed of thin, narrow scales which *curve outward from the trunk* at the ends. Younger trees have smooth gray bark. Terminal winter buds are large and cream colored with brown protective scales.

Hickory wood is noted for its strength. It was used for wagon spokes in the past. Now it is used for handles for axes and tools, for sporting goods, for lumber and firewood, and in the production of hickory smoked hams.

greatly reduced leaf

57

greatly reduced

1. winter branchlet showing buds
2. nut with husk removed
3. leaf scar with bud (enlarged)
4. branch with mature leaf and fruit
5. male catkins

MOCKERNUT HICKORY

Carya tomentosa Nutt.
Walnut Family

This is a large tree up to 80 feet in height which is not common in northern New England. It does grow in Vermont, but is more common farther south — especially in Massachusetts. It prefers rich, moist woods and requires sunlight. It is found mainly in valleys and in fertile soil at the bottom of slopes.

The alternate, fragrant, compound leaves are from 8-12 inches long with from 7-9 narrow leaflets which have toothed margins and are hairy on the underside. The upper pair of leaflets is the largest — with the greatest width nearer the point than the base of the leaflet. The leafstalks are hairy, flattened, grooved, and enlarged at the base.

The male flowers are in catkins which are in sets of three. The female flowers are in 2-4 flowered clusters.

The grayish or brownish, thick-shelled, 4-ribbed nut is enclosed in a thick reddish-brown, deeply 4-grooved husk which is depressed at the tip. This husk splits nearly to the base when ripe. The kernel inside is sweet to eat, but is small and rather hard to extract.

The bark is dark or light gray, thick and close — not shaggy. It is roughened by irregular furrows between rounded rather scaly ridges. The twigs — compared to the other hickories — are very stout and hairy and are quite fragrant when bruised. New growth is especially hairy. Twigs are reddish-brown with numerous long marks (lenticels). The pith is angular.

The buds have scales which are large, hairy, and overlapping. The terminal bud is much larger than the others. It has overlapping, hairy scales — the other pair of which drops off in autumn. The side buds are reddish-brown and do not split open early.

The wood is heavy, hard, and strong and is used commercially — often being sold as Shagbark Hickory. It makes a good fuel.

SWEET PIGNUT or PIGNUT HICKORY

Carya glabra (Mill.) Sweet
Walnut Family

enlarged twig showing
buds and leaf scar

reduced leaf

This hickory is a medium-sized tree usually 50-60 feet in height with a long, clean trunk and a narrow, oblong crown. It is most common on dry ridges and hillsides. It prefers plenty of sunshine.

The compound leaves are 8-12 inches long and have 5-7 toothed and pointed leaflets. These are rather thick and are dark green above and paler below. The leaflets are oblong and smooth.

The flowers are in catkins — male and female are separate — and appear when the leaves are about half developed. They are similar to the flowers on the preceding species.

The fruit is a nut with a pale brown, thick, bony shell which contains a kernel that is at first sweet, but becomes bitter. It is enclosed in a pear-shaped reddish-brown husk which may remain closed or may split open from the tip towards the middle.

The tough bark rarely peels off. It is close to the trunk, is dark gray, and has shallow fissures and narrow ridges. The newer twigs are smooth, slender and yellow green, but later become reddish-brown and are roughened by long, pale marks (lenticels), leaf scars, and bud scales. Terminal buds are short and stout with blunt tips. They are covered with reddish-brown scales with pale, silky inner scales. Sometimes the outer scales will drop off during the winter. The leaf scars are heart-shaped or three lobed with noticeable bundle scars.

The valuable wood is hard, strong, and similar to other hickories. It is used for handles, tools, fuel and for smoking meat.

Carya ovalis Wang Sarg is similar to *C. glabra*, but the husk on the nut splits freely to the base where it does not split to the base on *C. glabra*. *Carya ovalis* is found in southern New England. There are several varieties which vary slightly.

1. female flowers
2. male flowers in catkins

AMERICAN HAZELNUT or FILBERT
Corylus americana Walt.
Hazel Family

Hazelnut is a shrub 3-8 feet tall which occurs in clumps and often forms thickets. It grows in borders of woods, on hillsides, in thickets, and near open stone walls. Identifying characteristics are the unique nuts and the *pink hairs* which are at right angles to the twigs.

The broad, oval leaves have a pointed tip; irregular, toothed margins; and a base which may be either heart-shaped or rounded. Each leaf is on a short leaf stalk. The upper surface is dull, dark green and rough, but the underside is paler in color and covered with downy hairs.

The male flowers are in catkins which are usually single, but may be in groups of three. These are formed in the fall and open in the spring before the leaves do. The female flowers are small and develop from short, scaly buds. These have crimson stigmas which project from the center.

The fruit is a globular chestnut-brown nut surrounded by two leafy, hairy green bracts with fringed margins. The nut is about ½ inch long, slightly flattened, and roughened at its base where the leafy bracts were attached.

The bark is smooth, thin, and dark brown. The twigs are gray to russet-brown, smooth, and covered with pinkish hairs which are at right angles to the twigs.

The wood is not used commercially, but the nuts are greatly prized and picked to be sold at the market.

BEAKED HAZELNUT
Corylus cornuta (rostrata) Marsh.
Hazel Family

Beaked Hazelnut is a northern shrub which is usually from 3-8 feet high and has several stems. It is common along roadsides, in rich thickets, clearings, and at borders of woods.

The alternate, simple leaves are broadly-oval and abruptly taper to a point. The base of the leaf may be heartshaped or almost scallop-lobed with these lobes nearly overlapping at the stalk. The margins of the leaves are doubly-toothed with the longest points being at the *tips of the veins.* The leaves are a dull, dark green, are deeply seamed above, and densely velvety-hairy and prominently ribbed beneath.

The fruit is an edible, sweet, ovoid nut which is enclosed in a densely-bristly covering that terminates in a long, tubular beak. These nuts are often in groups of two or three.

The bark is a light ocher-yellow or brown-ocher dotted with buff. The young twigs are ocher and — seen through a hand lens — covered with a fine hairiness.

reduced

EASTERN HOPHORNBEAM or IRONWOOD

Ostrya virginiana (Mill.) K. Koch
Birch Family

Eastern Hophornbeam is a small tree with a trunk fluted — similar to, but not as ribbed as Blue Beech — usually not more than 10 or 12 inches in diameter at the trunk and seldom more than thirty feet in height. The branches are long and slender and have drooping tips. It grows best in rich or rocky woods and on warm slopes with gravelly soil.

The alternate, oval leaves are pointed at both ends. They have sharply-double toothed margins and are widest at the middle of the leaf. The leaf blades may be from 2-4 inches long and are hairy on both surfaces. There are *tufts of hair* in the axils of the veins on the underside of the leaf.

Male catkins are formed in the fall, usually in clusters of three at the tips of the twigs. These appear in May before the leaves, and lengthen as they mature.

The fruit is a hop-like cluster of bladdery sacs, each of which encloses a small, flat, smooth seed-like nutlet.

The bark is thin and gray with long flaky scales which *lift up from both edges* but hold fast in the middle. These scales become finer and stringier as the tree ages. The twigs are light brown, tough, and wiry with a green pith.

The wood is hard and strong, but the trees are mostly too small to be useful. The wood is suitable for wedges, mallets, and commercial rollers, and it is a very good fuel.

BLUE BEECH;
AMERICAN HORNBEAM;
IRONWOOD

Carpinus caroliniana Walt.
Birch Family

Blue Beech is a small tree — often growing in clusters or in a leaning position — which can readily be identified by the smooth, blue-gray bark with wavy, twisting, bluish or grey *bands or ribs which run vertically on the trunk.* It is a slow-growing tree which rarely gets taller than thirty feet. It grows in rich woods in moist, shady ground and especially along streams and at the edges of swamps.

The simple, alternate leaves may be from 2-3 inches (2.5-8 cm.) long and are smooth above and hairy below. The sides of the leaf blade run parallel for a distance before tapering to a point. Leaf margins are sharply double-toothed and the tiny teeth almost look like a fringe. Blue Beech leaves turn a brilliant scarlet in autumn.

The flower catkins of spring develop into a distinctive fruit. It is an open, drooping cluster of stiff, three-lobed, leaf-like bracts with *ribbed, seed-like nutlets* in the center. These clusters hang on the trees long after leaves have fallen in autumn.

The strong, thin branches are rather crooked. They reach out horizontally, but support many graceful, drooping branchlets. The twigs are reddish-brown, slender, and tough. Buds are slender, reddish-brown, sharp-pointed, and covered with from 8-12 visible bud scales. The scales are keeled and give the bud *a distinctive squarish look.*

The wood is close-grained, compact, strong, tough, and durable — hence the name of Ironwood. It is used for handles, levers, and fuel.

enlarged bud
showing
keeled scales

cone-like fruit

The alternate, simple leaves may occur singly or in pairs from the same point. They usually have heart-shaped bases, toothed margins, and long-pointed tips. They are dark green above, pale green below, and from 2½ to 5 inches in length.

There are two kinds of flowers. The male catkins form in the fall in clusters of three which elongate to three or four inches the following spring. The pale green female flowers are in slender spikes which are ½-1 inch (1.5-2.5 cm.) long. These mature to a long, smooth, cone-like structure with small, three-lobed scales holding small winged nutlets.

The bark of this birch *does not peel off* in layers. Bark on older trees is distinctly black and broken into large, thick irregular plates which are smooth on the surface. Bark on younger trees is smooth, shining, reddish-brown, and covered with horizontally-elongated marks (lenticels). Young twigs are light green and hairy, but later become smooth, reddish-brown and shiny. They have a *strong wintergreen flavor.* Winter buds are shiny, long, sharp-pointed, and covered with reddish-brown, overlapping scales.

The wood is heavy, strong, hard and dark brown. It is used for furniture where it is sometimes substituted for mahogany, cherry, or hickory. It takes a high polish readily. It makes a superb firewood.

BLACK BIRCH or SWEET BIRCH
Betula lenta L.
Birch Family

Black Birch is usually fifty or sixty feet tall, but does reach heights up to eighty feet. The trunk is sometimes subdivided. On young trees the lateral branches form a narrow, conical crown, but on older trees, the branches may be more pendulous to form a wide-spreading crown. Black Birch grows in rich soil on dry slopes, but is also found on rocky mountain slopes.

YELLOW BIRCH
Betula lutea Michx.
Birch Family

Yellow Birch is a large forest tree which is usually sixty to eighty feet high, but occasionally reaches heights up to one hundred feet. The short trunk often branches near the base, and the slender branches form a

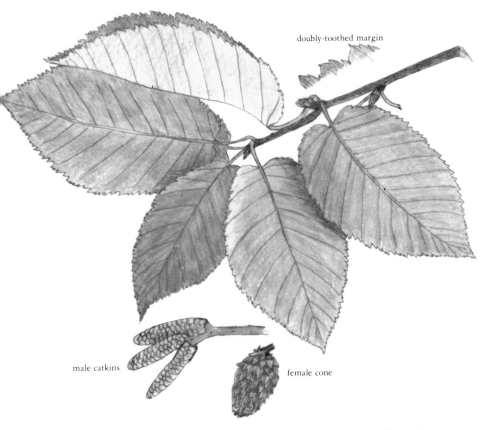

doubly-toothed margin

male catkins

female cone

wide, open, hemispherical crown. It is common on moist, rich uplands, along borders of streams, or near swamps.

The simple leaves are heartshaped at the base, are from two to four inches long, and are *doubly-toothed* on the margins. (See insert). The leaves may occur singly, or in pairs originating at the same point, but *are never opposite*. They are dull green on the top and yellow-green below, and have more than eight veins.

Flowers of two kinds usually appear on the same branch. Male catkins form in the fall, remain on all winter, and lengthen and mature in the spring. The female flower is more cone-like and matures in July. These "seed cones"

are light brown and hairy, and remain on the tree for several months.

The bark has a silverish-yellow sheen to it. It is thin, rather loose, and *peels laterally* in thin layers. The twigs (when broken) have a pleasant wintergreen flavor. The slender twigs are first green and hairy, but turn yellow or brown as they mature. The elongated horizontal marks (called lenticels) will in time unite to form a continuous horizontal line. Winter buds are downy.

The yellow birch wood is yellowish, heavy, hard, and strong. It is a valuable wood which is prized mostly for veneer, but is also used for lumber, flooring, furniture, and wooden bowls. It makes a superior firewood.

4.

1. section of winter branch showing buds and leaf scar
2. an enlarged winged seed
3. an enlarged scale from the strobile
4. flowering twig with female flowers and male catkins

RED or RIVER BIRCH

Betula nigra L.
Birch Family

River Birch is a medium-sized tree usually 30-50 feet in height, but occasionally grows to 80 feet. The trunk is usually short and is often divided near the base into several arching limbs. The crown is rather narrow and is very irregular. It prefers the banks of streams, rivers, lakes and swamps, but is occasionally found in drier locations.

The bright green leaves occur singly or in pairs from the same point on the twig, but are not opposite. The leaf stalk and lower surface of the blade is hairy. The blades are 1-2 inches wide, are unevenly double-toothed at the margins, and have pointed tips.

The base of the leaf blade is distinctive on Red Birch. It is broad-angled and essentially free from teeth in the basal area.

The female flowers are in short-stemmed cylindrical *erect catkins* which develop in the spring from buds below the hanging male catkins. Male catkins form in the fall and elongate in the spring to 2-3 inches.

The fruit is an erect, hairy, cylindrical strobile 1-1½ inches long. It is made up of many 3-lobed hairy scales fastened to a central axis and bearing small, hairy, winged nuts.

The bark on lower parts of older trunks is reddish-brown and is roughened by fissures which separate into irregular scales. The bark on younger trees or the upper parts of older trees peels off in thin, film-like papery scales which are red-brown in color and persist for a few years. During this time, the scales become fringed and expose the light, lustrous red bark underneath.

The twigs are slender, green and hairy at first, but later become smooth, reddish brown, and bear horizontal marks called lenticels. The buds are sharp-pointed, shining brown or slightly hairy, and are covered with 3-7 chestnut-brown, overlapping scales.

The wood is light, soft, strong, and is used for furniture, wooden ware, fruit and vegetable baskets.

GRAY BIRCH
Betula populifolia Marsh.
Birch Family

   Gray Birch is a small, rather bushy tree which rarely gets taller than thirty feet. It often occurs in clumps and is usually in a leaning position. It is quite abundant in southern New England and not as common in northern Maine. It is a short-lived tree which is of little value. It grows in sterile soil of old fields, in burns, or in heavily-cut areas.

   The simple, alternate leaves are dark green, somewhat lustrous, and triangular in general outline. The base is flat and the tip is long and tapering. Each is on a short leaf stalk, is from 2½ to 3 inches in length, and has doubly-toothed margins. The slightest breeze causes them to flutter like the leaves on poplars — hence the Latin name which means "birch with popular-like leaves."

   The flowers are produced in catkins. Male catkins appear in the fall and are *usually solitary*. They are 1½-2½ inches long during the winter and lengthen to 2-4 inches in the spring. The female flowers are in slender, cylindrical spikes about ½ inch long, but lengthening to an inch (2.5 cm.) when in fruit. The fruit has thin wings which are broader than the nutlet.

   The bark is close and firm and *does not easily peel into thin layers*. The outer part is chalky-white with dark, elongated markings. The inner part is orange. There are *black triangular blotches* below each lateral branch. The branches are often in a hanging position. The slender twigs are tough and wiry, and have a *rough, warty surface*. Buds are sharp-pointed and point away from the twig. Each is covered with three or four visible brown scales with downy margins.

   The wood is light, soft, and decays rapidly when exposed. It is used for paper-roll plugs, pulpwood, and fuel — if it is dried well and kept under cover.

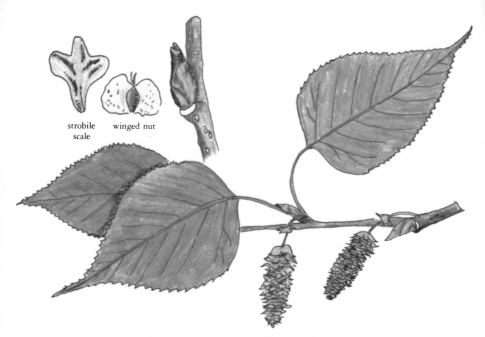

strobile
scale

winged nut

BLUE BIRCH

Betula caerulea-grandis Blanch.
Birch Family

    Blue Birch is a large tree up to 65 feet in height. It resembles White Birch, and it is difficult to distinguish the two. Blue Birch has a creamy-white to pinkish-white bark which comes off in layers. The branches and twigs are loosely spreading and are slightly pendulous. It grows in dry woods of northern New England.

    The leaves are a lustrous blue-green, and are broadly egg-shaped with a long-pointed tip and a rounded base. They are usually 2-4 inches (6-10 cm.) long and may be slightly hairy on the veins and midrib on the underside. The margins are coarsely-toothed, *except at the base near the leaf stalk.*

    The male flowers are in catkins which are usually in a cluster. The female flower develops into a hairy strobile about one inch long. This is made up of three-lobed bracts, each of which having a nut that is much narrower than its wings.

The young twigs on this birch are usually hairy. This is an identifying characteristic.

DWARF WHITE BIRCH
Betula minor (Tuckerm.) Fern.
Birch Family

Dwarf White Birch is a shrub which varies greatly in size. It may be less than a foot tall or may reach heights more than 6 feet. It is found only in ravines and on alpine summits of higher mountains in northern New England. The tough branches have dark, close bark. Newer branchlets often bear light-colored warts. The pointed leaves resemble those on Heart-Leaved White Birch, but are smaller. They vary in size from 1-2 inches in length and may be either rounded or wedge-shaped at the base. The margins have rather large teeth compared to the size of the leaf blade. The leaves are not hairy, and grow in pairs from short projections on the twigs. The catkins may be form ¾ to 2 inches in length, depending on the size of the shrub and the maturity of the catkins. These flower in June.

male catkin
in fall

PAPER or WHITE BIRCH
Betula papyrifera Marsh.
Birch Family

White Birch is usually sixty or seventy feet in height, but occasionally reaches heights up to eighty feet. Trees in the open quite often develop in groups of three or four. These "clumps" are highly prized as lawn trees. Birches grow along streams, lakes and ponds where soil is rich and moist, but are also found scattered through forests. The Shelburne Birches in New Hampshire are beautiful examples of White Birch trees.

The simple, alternate, egg-shaped, short-pointed leaves are thicker than those of the gray birch. They are doubly-toothed at the margins and have a dull, dark green upper surface. The leaf base may be either round or heart-shaped.

Female flowers are in catkins 1-2 inches (2.5-6.5 cm.) long, with light green, pointed scales and bright red styles and may appear singly or in clusters along the twigs. The male catkins form in the fall — usually in groups of two or three at the tips of the branchlets. These mature in the spring and lengthen to about four inches.

The bark on the trunk and larger limbs separates freely and easily into thin, papery sheets. The outer surface is white while the inner surface is orange. Black or orange horizontally-elongated lenticels mark both surfaces. This bark is a protective layer and *should never be removed* from living trees. The twigs are rather stout, are usually hairy, and have no wintergreen flavor. *Buds are sharp-pointed, slightly sticky,* and are covered with a few overlapping scales.

The wood is fairly hard, strong, but not too heavy. It is used for clothespins, woodenware, spools, toys, dowels, etc. It is also used for plywood, pulp and firewood. Paper Birch sap may be gathered in the spring and boiled down to make a syrup much like that from maple trees.

HEART-LEAVED WHITE BIRCH

Betula papyrifera var. *cordifolia* (Regel) Fern.
Birch Family

This birch is very similar to White Birch, but the leaves are definitely heart-shaped at the base. The bracts of the mature female catkins are longer, and the bark of mature trunks is red-brown to creamy- or pinkish-white.

It is common only on mountains above 2000 feet in altitude where it generally replaces the Paper or White Birch of lower elevations. It is a small to medium tree or large shrub when it is growing in unsheltered locations.

NORTHERN BIRCH

Betula borealis Spach
(not shown)
Birch Family

This birch resembles Dwarf White Birch, but the *young leaves will be hairy.* Northern Birch may be an upright to depressed shrub or a small shrubby tree; it has been found growing on Mt. Katahdin in Maine and in northern Vermont.

The new branchlets and sprouts are hairy, and the bark is close-fitting and dark-colored. The short-stalked leaves are broadly-oval with a pointed tip. Leaves on fertile branches are 1-2½ inches (1.5-5.5 cm.) long. The margins are toothed. Though young leaves are hairy, mature leaves may be quite hairless.

BOG or LOW BIRCH
Betula pumila L.
Birch Family

This is a variable birch. It may be an erect shrub 1½ to 10 feet (.5-3 m.) in height or may be matted or lying flat on the ground. It usually grows in sphagnous areas, but it may also be found in wooded swamps — especially if calcium is present in the soil. The young branchlets are usually quite hairy, but may be nearly smooth on some shrubs. Branchlets may be glandless or have a few glandular dots. The alternate, simple leaves are rather roundish with coarsely-toothed margins, and both surfaces of the leaf will have a noticeable network of veins. Most leaves will be pale green to whitish and hairy on the underside. Leaves vary in length from ½ to 2½ inches (.8-7 cm.). The male catkins form in autumn and remain on the tree all winter. The female catkins form on the tips of short new shoots in the spring. The fruiting catkins are erect and thick. The winged fruit is nearly round with wings barely as wide as the nutlet. These mature in the fall.

ALPINE or DWARF BIRCH
Betula glandulosa Michx.
Birch Family

Alpine Birch is not common, but is found in several alpine areas on the higher mountains of northern New England. It is a low or trailing shrub which may stand upright to heights up to 2 feet, but is more often matted and pressed close to the ground. The leaves are small and nearly round, with *scalloped teeth on the margins*. The leaves are thick and bright green on both sides. They vary in size from ¼ to 1¼ inches in length. Young branchlets are usually not hairy. Older branches are brown and are conspicuously dotted with resinous wart-like glands. The catkins flower in June and may be ½ to 1 inch in length.

MOUNTAIN ALDER
Alnus crispa (Ait.) Pursh
Birch Family

Mountain Alder a shrub up to six feet in height, and is the only alder found on mountains. It ascends to 5000 feet on Mt. Washington. It is common on mountains throughout northern New England, but occasionally it is found in lowlands along rocky banks of streams or on coastal ledges.

The alternate leaves are simple with rather long leaf stalks. They may be from two to four inches in length, and have a rounded base and fine-toothed margins. The edge of the leaves sometimes are slightly ruffled. The underside of the leaf may be smooth or hairy, has *prominent rusty veins*, and is rather rough in texture.

The yellow-green male catkins are about 1½ inches long and bloom before the leaves are fully out. The female flowers are cone-like and about one inch long. They appear in April or May, but remain on the tree all winter.

The smooth brown bark has small indistinct white spots on it. The *buds are not stalked* as they are in the Speckled Alder. The tree has little value. It is a pioneer plant on landslides, in gravel areas, and in abandoned fields along the coast.

SPECKLED ALDER
Alnus rugosa (Du Roi) Spreng.
Birch Family

Speckled Alder is a common shrub or small tree seldom more than twenty feet tall. It usually grows in wet places along brooks, in swamps, and in unkept pastures. It sprouts readily and grows in large clumps which will soon overtake pastureland if not cut down. The alternate leaves are 2-3 inches (5-8 cm.) in length and have a rough texture. The blade is broadly oval with unevenly toothed or doubly-toothed margins. The base of the leaf is rounded or somewhat narrowed.

The flowers are in catkins and open before the leaves do in the spring. The purplish, wax-like male catkins are formed in late summer or fall. The female catkin develops into a woody, cone-like structure on a short stem.

The bark is smooth, dark chocolate brown marked with white elongated spots called lenticels. The twigs are reddish brown. If a twig is cut, the pith inside will be in a triangular shape. *Winter buds are born on stalks.*

The alder has little value, except perhaps as a soil holder on banks and along streams. Woodcock abound where there are many alders.

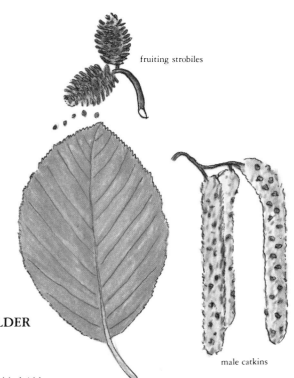

fruiting strobiles

male catkins

COMMON or SMOOTH ALDER

Alnus serrulata (Ait.) Willd.
Birch Family

This alder is very similar to Speckled Alder. It is usually about fifteen feet tall and is found in swamps, on banks of streams, and along shores. The female blossom develops into an erect fruiting cone, and the male flowers are in slender, drooping catkins which mature in early spring before the leaves do.

Distinguishing characteristics for this alder are:

1. The leaves are green underneath — not pale as in Speckled Alder. The underside is not hairy.

2. The margins of the leaf on this alder are finely saw-toothed — not doubly-toothed.

3. The base of the leaf is wedge-shaped — not rounded or heart-shaped, and the leaf blade is broadest at or about the middle.

4. Winter buds are stalked.

AMERICAN BEECH
Fagus grandifolia Ehrh.
Beech Family

Beech is a large tree usually abut 60 or 70 feet in height, but occasionally up to 125 feet It is found on rich, moist bottom lands and also on gravelly slopes and rich uplands where it tends to form pure stands. It is rare in limestone valleys.

The alternate, simple, leathery leaves are oval with sharp-toothed margins. The leaves feel rather stiff and dry like parchment. The leaves are a lighter yellow-green on the under surface, and each *vein ends at the tip of a tooth*

Flowers appear in April before the leaves are all opened. Male flowers are in a fluffy stalked, round head about an inch in diameter Female flowers occur in two-flowered clusters in the axils of upper leaves. The fruit is a stalked, four-valved bur with weak spines. It contains two or three pale brown, triangular-shaped nuts with a sweet edible kernel. These nuts mature in one season and are valuable as food for wildlife.

The bark is very close, smooth, and light gray with dark spots. The twigs are slender, yellow-gray, hairy at first but later becoming smooth. The twigs are rather zigzag and are covered with yellowish marks and marked with old leaf scars. The buds are very long, slender, and sharp-pointed with reddish-brown scales. There is usually a terminal bud present.

The wood is hard, strong, tough, but not durable. It is difficult to dry and season, but when dry makes a good firewood. Beech is used for railroad ties, pulpwood, veneer, parquet flooring, furniture, novelty wares, carpenter tools, and charcoal.

AMERICAN CHESTNUT
Castanea dentata (Marsh.) Borkh.
Beech Family

American Chestnut is a tall and stately tree with a massive trunk and a broad top. It used to be found growing to heights of eighty or more feet, but now is rarely found bigger than sprout growth less than twenty feet. An imported fungus struck the trees at their tops and slowly moved downward to kill the tree by inches. Scientists tried in vain to save the trees. Saplings which now sprout from older, dead trunks soon get the disease and die. Chestnut grows in good soil in pastures and rocky woods and is more common in southern New England.

The rather dry, stiff-textured leaves are similar to beech leaves but are longer and narrower. The alternate, simple leaves have hook-like sharp teeth at their margins. The veins are straight, and each vein terminates in a tooth. The leaves are yellow green and smooth on both surfaces, and have points at both ends.

The male flowers are in erect catkins, making the tree tops fuzzy and pale when they are in bloom.

The fruits are beautiful, shiny-brown, wedge-shaped nuts. Two or three of these nuts are enclosed in a prickly bur which is from two to three inches in diameter. The bur lining is plush-like, and each nut is tipped with fuzz or hairs.

Bark on old trees is dark brown and divided into broad, flat ridges by shallow, irregular fissures. The bark on saplings is smooth, dark gray, and has a greenish tinge.

The wood is soft and very durable — due to tannic acid which is found in it. Before the blight hit, chestnut wood was highly prized for telephone poles, railroad ties, and fence posts. The nuts were gathered in great quantities for the market.

OAKS
Beech Family

Oaks are mighty trees, and there are abou fifteen different kinds found in New England These may hybridize and cause identification problems for a beginner.

Our native oaks fall into two divisions — the white oaks and the black oaks. White oak produce mature acorns in a single season while acorns on black oaks are not mature until the second season. Another difference is that the lobes of the leaves of white oaks are no bristle-tipped, while the leaf lobes of black oaks are terminated by bristles. For completely safe indentification, one needs to see the bark, the leaf, and the acorn.

The identifying characteristics are given for ten oaks in this book. For more technical data please consult Gray's *Manual of Botany* or other similar books.

WHITE OAKS
Quercus alba L.
Beech Family

White Oak probably gets its name from its pale bark and leaves. It is a very large and variable tree, usually 70 or 80 feet tall but occasionally up to 140 feet in height. It may be found growing in many habitats, but it grows best in rich, moist, rather heavy soil of uplands.

The simple, alternate leaves are from 4-9 inches long and have from 3-9 lobes, *usually 7*. The lobes have *no bristle tip*, and are rather bluntly-rounded. The leaves are bright green above, but are a paler green underneath. The leaves sometimes remain on the tree all winter.

The cylindrical acorns are about ¾ of an inch in length and the warty, shallow cup only covers the lower quarter (sometimes third) of the acorn.

On smaller branches, the bark is light green to reddish green, but on mature trunks may be up to 2 inches thick and is light gray or white. It has flat irregular flakes separated by shallow fissures. The twigs are gray to purple. Buds are blunt-pointed and have scales with no hairs. Terminal buds are clustered.

The wood is strong, heavy, hard, and durable. It is used in construction, shipbuilding, furniture, posts, piling, flooring, interior finish of houses, fences, and for fuel.

BUR or MOSSY-CUP OAK
Quercus macrocarpa Michx.
Beech Family

Bur Oak grows in low, rich bottom lands and is rarely found in dry soil. It reaches heights of 60 to 70 feet, has a broad top with wide-spreading branches and a trunk which may be branchless the first two-thirds or more of its length.

The simple, alternate leaves are *voilin-shaped* in general outline. The lobes are rounded, but not as deeply cut as those on White Oak. The upper end of the leaf is usually the widest. The upper surface is dark green and shiny, while the underside is pale green or silvery white. Many leaves have a typical pair of deep sinuses near the middle. (See insert.)

The acorn matures the first year, and is usually solitary on the twigs. The acorn varies much in size and shape, but it is generally ¾ inch long and is at least half-covered by the cup. The margin of the cup is *fringed with long, hair-like scales*. The fruit is edible.

The bark is grayish and is deeply furrowed and broken into irregular, plate-like scales. The twigs have corky wings or ridges.

The wood is very durable, heavy, strong, and hard. It is used for boatbuilding, tools, interior finish, railroad ties, posts, piling, and poles. It makes a good firewood.

1. twig with mature leaves and long-stalked acorns
2. a winter twig with buds, lenticels, leaf scars and 5-sided pith
3. a cluster of male blossoms

SWAMP WHITE OAK
Quercus bicolor Willd.
Beech Family

Swamp White Oak is a medium sized tree usually 50-70 feet high, but it occasionally reaches heights of nearly 100 feet. It can be distinguished from the other oaks by the peeling branches and the shallow clefts between the lobes on the leaf. The scraggy and peeling branches make this tree rather unattractive for use as an ornamental. It generally grows in the moist or swampy soil of lowlands.

The simple, alternate leaves are narrow at the base and broader at and beyond the middle. The leaves are usually 5-6 inches long and the margin is irregularly and shallowly lobed. The top surface is a deep, shiny, olive green and the underside is densely white-woolly.

The male flowers are in hairy catkins 4-5 inches long. Female flowers are on short stalks and may be either solitary or in small clusters.

The oval, chestnut-red acorns are usually in pairs on a long stalk. Each acorn is about 1 inch (2-3 cm.) long and has a woody, scaly, somewhat fringed cup one-third to one-half as long as the acorn. The cup is deeply saucer-shaped and is hairy on the inside.

The bark is dark-brown to black and is coarsely ridged, furrowed, or scaled on the upper branches. Bark on younger trees is a warm light brown, but bark on older stems is ragged or shredded. Newer twigs are yellowish to reddish-brown, usually smooth, and covered with pale, raised marks called lenticels. The pith is 5-angled as in other oaks. Buds are broadly egg-shaped with scales and a blunt tip. They may have some hairs towards the tip.

The wood is strong, heavy, and hard and has the same uses as White Oak.

YELLOW or CHINKAPIN OAK
Quercus muehlenbergii Engelm.
Beech Family

This oak is a beautiful tree to plant as an ornamental. It is usually 50-80 feet in height, but occasionally it is more than 100 feet in places south of New England. In this area, it is not abundant, and when found, the tree is apt to be stunted in growth. The trunk is often buttressed at the base and the crown is narrow, shallow, and round-topped. This oak grows best in dry, rocky soils, especially in limestone soil.

The simple, alternate leaves are oblong from 4-7 inches long. They have coarse, bluntly-pointed marginal teeth and slender leaf stalks. The under surface has fine white hairs and the upper surface is dark green and shiny. The leaves of this tree resemble those of the Chestnut Oak except that the tip is much more acute.

The male flowers occur in hairy catkins 3-4 inches long and appear when the leaves are about one-third developed. The female flowers develop from buds in the axils of upper leaves. These flowers have bright red stigmas.

The small acorns are no more than an inch long at most, and are usually not on stalks. The lower half of the acorn is in a bowl-shaped cup. The thin tips of the scales form a fringe around the margin of the cup.

The bark is thick and rough, and has long fissures separated by irregular, scaly ridges. The twigs are slender, red-brown to gray-brown and hairy at first, but later becoming smooth with pale marks (lenticels). The pith is star shaped. Buds are oval and pointed, and are covered with overlapping scales which are slightly hairy along the margins.

The wood is heavy, hard, strong, and durable when in contact with the soil. It is used for the same purposes as White Oak, except that it is not good for cabinets as it tends to check badly. It makes an excellent fuel.

DWARF or
SCRUB CHESTNUT OAK
Quercus prinoides Willd.
Beech Family

This oak is a low shrub 2-6 feet high but occasionally reaches heights up to 18 feet. It usually occurs in clumps, but may be solitary. It prefers dry woods, rocky slopes, or sandy soils but is occasionally found in hillside pasture and moist woodlands.

The simple, alternate leaves are 2-5 inches (5-12 cm.) long on short, stout leaf stalks. From 3-7 rounded teeth are on each margin and the tip is somewhat pointed. The leaves are bright green above and white-woolly beneath.

The male flowers are in catkins similar to the Swamp White Oak. These catkins are yellow, hairy, and 1½ to 2½ inches (4-6.5 cm. long. The female flowers are hairy, on short stalks, and have bright red pistils.

Many small acorns ½ to ¾ inches (1-2 cm.) long are produced either singly or in pairs. These may have a short stalk or none at all. The oval nut is blunt pointed and a shiny brown, except at the tip where it may be covered with pale down. The *kernel is sweet and edible.* The cup covers one-half of the acorn.

The bark is thin and light brown and is marked with light gray blotches. At first it is smooth, but if the trunk reaches a diameter of four inches or so, then the bark will be rough. The twigs are slender, dark green and hairy at first, but later become reddish-brown dotted with pale marks (lenticels). The light brown buds are round at the tip and are covered with overlapping scales.

The tree is so small that it is not commercially important. It is hard wood, however, and may be used locally as firewood.

1. enlarged winter twig
2. enlarged male flower
3. enlarged female flower
4. an acorn cup

ROCK or CHESTNUT OAK
Quercus prinus L.
Beech Family

winter twig

This oak belongs in the White Oak group. It is a medium-sized tree usually 60-70 feet in height but occasionally reaches heights up to 100 feet. In dense stands, the trunk is straight and continuous, while in the open it is low and divided with a very broad, open crown. It is usually found on dry hillsides. It can be distinguished from other oaks by its oblong leaves with margins of coarse, rounded teeth and the roughly fissured, non-scaly bark.

The alternate, simple, stiff or leathery leaves are from 5-9 inches (1-2 dm.) long. Usually they have a narrow wedge-shaped base with the widest part above the middle of the blade. They are green and smooth on the top surface, but pale green (at first) and hairy on the lower surface.

The flowers appear when the leaves are about one-third developed. Yellow male flowers are in hairy catkins 2-3 inches (5-8 cm.) long. The female flowers occur in small clusters, are on stout stalks, and have a short, divergent, reddish style protruding from the center.

The acorn may be solitary or in pairs and matures in one season. The nut is 4/5 to 1½ inches (2-3 cm.) long and is 2-3 times as long as it is broad. It contains a sweet, edible kernel. The cup is thin, hairy on the inside, and covers only one-third of the nut.

Bark on young stems is smooth, thin, and yellowish brown. On older branches and the trunk, it is rough, brown to black, and is divided into broad and continuous fissures which separate the sharp-angled ridges. The base of the fissures are cinnamon-red —

especially on larger branches. Winter twigs are slender, angular, orange-brown and terminated by a cluster of buds. The buds are sharp-pointed and conical with overlapping scales which are hairy on the tips. The wood is heavy, strong, and durable when in contact with soil. It is used for railroad ties, fencing, fuel and construction.

83

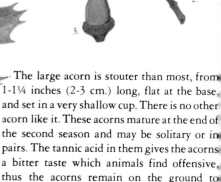

1. first year acorns
2. mature acorns
3. acorn on *Quercus rubra* var. *borealis*

NORTHERN RED OAK

Quercus rubra L.
Beech Family

Red Oak is a tall, handsome tree about 70-80 feet tall which occasionally grows to 150 feet. It has a straight trunk which is clear of branches for some distance above the ground. It prefers porous sandy soil of uplands and will not grow in wet soil.

The leaves vary considerably in size and shape. They may be from 5-9 inches (1-2 dm.) long but have many lobes which are bristle-tipped. They are deep green above with a yellowish or red midrib and yellowish green with a yellow midrib on the underside. The shape of the leaf blade is broadly oval with V-shaped sinuses or cuts between the pointed lobes. These cuts are never more than half way to the midrib. Because of the variability of the leaves, the acorn is better to use for identification purposes.

The large acorn is stouter than most, from 1-1¼ inches (2-3 cm.) long, flat at the base, and set in a very shallow cup. There is no other acorn like it. These acorns mature at the end of the second season and may be solitary or in pairs. The tannic acid in them gives the acorns a bitter taste which animals find offensive, thus the acorns remain on the ground to produce saplings in great numbers. Acorns of *Quercus rubra* var. *borealis* have a narrower, longer nut in a deep cup. The base of the cup is not flat.

Bark on young stems and branches is gray to brown. On older trunks it is thick, broken up by fissures into regular, continuous, dark brown and distinctly flat-topped ridges. The twigs are rather slender, smooth, greenish-brown to dark brown and covered with pale, indistinct markings. The buds are brown, smooth, and pointed.

The wood is heavy, strong, hard, close-grained and a light reddish-brown. It is our most important timber oak in northern New England and is used for flooring, interior finish, railroad ties, plywood, furniture, and construction, and is excellent for fuel when dry.

SCARLET OAK

Quercus coccinea Muenchh.
Beech Family

1. winter twig showing leaf scar and hairy buds
2. immature acorns
3. mature acorns

Scarlet Oak is a medium-sized tree usually 60-80 feet but it occasionally reaches heights up to 150 feet. The lower branches often droop down. The trunk is tapered and the crown is narrow and shallow. It is not common in northern New England, but grows in dry shady or rocky soils in southern New England.

The simple leaves are alternate, have long stalks, and are from 3-6 inches (.7-1.5 dm.) long. There are from 5-9 bristle-tipped lobes which are separated by deep, rounded spaces (sinuses) that are at least two-thirds the distance from the tip to the midrib. The leaves turn scarlet in fall.

The flowers appear in May when the leaves are one-third developed. Male flowers are in slender, hairy catkins 3-4 inches long. Female flowers are reddish and are on short, hairy stalks.

The reddish-brown acorn matures at the end of the second season. The acorns may be solitary or paired. The thin cup has flat, sharp-pointed, overlapping, shiny scales and usually covers one-half of the acorn. The tip of the acorn may be marked with circular lines.

Bark on old trunks has irregular, deep fissures which separate the ridges. The inner bark is red to gray. On younger limbs, the bark is thin, smooth and light brown. Twigs are slender, smooth, reddish or grayish brown, and are covered with small, pale marks. Brownish buds are hairy or woolly above the middle.

The wood is strong, heavy, and coarse. It is an excellent fuel when dry.

1. enlarged first year acorn
2. winter twig with hairy buds
3. mature acorns

BLACK OAK
Quercus velutina Lam.
Beech Family

Black Oak is a large oak which is usually 60-80 feet but may reach heights up to 150 feet with a trunk 4½ feet in diameter. Black Oak grows on dry uplands, gravelly plains, ridges, and foothills, and is seldom found in rich bottomlands.

There may be *many varieties of leaves on each tree.* The alternate, simple leaves are 4-8 inches (1-2.5 dm.) long and have 7 lobes which end in a bristle point. The rounded indentations (sinuses) between the lobes very greatly. Mature leaves are dark green and smooth above and pale to coppery green below with *tufts of rusty hairs* in the axils of veins at the midrib.

Male flowers are in hairy catkins 4-6 inches (1-1.5 dm) long. Female flowers are on short, hairy stalks. The acorn takes two years to mature. It may be solitary or clustered, and may or may not be on a stalk. The thin cup tapers at the base and covers one-half of the acorn. The scales on the cap are loose and dull.

Bark on young stems is smooth and dark brown, but soon becomes rough and black. On old trunks, the bark is very tough and thick, and is broken into deep fissures which separate the thick ridges. The *inner bark is yellow.* The twigs are stout, reddish-brown and are very angular. The twigs have pale marks (lenticels), may have rusty hairs, and have long ridges beginning at the leaf scars and running downward. The *twigs have a bitter taste.*

The buds are angled and are covered with overlapping bud scales which have yellowish or dirty-white hairs on them. This is very characteristic of Black Oak.

The wood is hard, heavy, and strong, but not tough, and it checks easily. It is used for furniture, interior finish, and construction.

BEAR or SCRUB OAK
Quercus ilicifolia Wang.
Beech Family

Bear Oak is a scrub oak which is rarely found north of southern or southeastern Maine. This oak is quite common on sand barrens where these intricately-branched, shrubby trees form almost impenetrable thickets. Bear Oak is usually less than twenty feet in height and is of little commercial value.

The simple, alternate leaves have only a few short, triangular lobes with a *bristle tip*. The leaves are a beautiful rich, bluish-green on top, but are whitish beneath with a fine mat of hairs. Leaves are 2-5 inches (5-12 cm.) in length. From a distance the leaves look similar to those on a holly tree, hence the Latin name which means holly-leaved.

Small acorns take two years to mature. They are about 2/5 inch (1 cm.) long with a cup about half as long as the nut. The cup is covered with closely overlapping scales. The acorn is rather pointed.

The bark is smooth and very dark; the branches are tough; and the winter buds are blunt-tipped.

1. enlarged leaf scar
2. enlarged winter twig with hairy bud
3. enlarged flower
4. mature fruit (samaras)

SLIPPERY or RED ELM

Ulmus rubra (Fulva) Muhl.
Elm Family

   Slippery Elm is usually 40-60 feet tall but may reach heights up to 80 feet. The crown is broad and flat-topped. The limbs are stout and curve upwards. It grows in low, rich soil along streams and also on hillsides, but is not common in northern New England. Slippery Elm can be distinguished from other elms by its fragrant and mucilaginous inner bark, by its dark brown winter buds which are covered with dusty brown hairs, and also by the position of the hairs on the fruits, which are on the central portion only.

88

The simple, alternate leaves are thick, rough, and pointed at the tip, and have a doubly-toothed margin. The base is rounded or *lop-sided*. The leaves are a deep olive green and are sometimes rusty-downy on the underside.

The flower buds are stout and are located along-side the twig, while the leaf buds are relatively slender and are located towards the tip of the twig. The yellowish flowers are clustered on short stalks and contain both male and female parts.

The fruit is a short-stalked samara which has a flat seed body surrounded by a wing. The samara is about ¾ inch (1-2 cm.) broad and is hairy over the seed only — not on the wings.

The bark is thick, rough, has long fissures and is dark brown tinged with red. The inner bark is fragrant and slippery. The twigs are stout and are difficult to break because of their flexibility. Young twigs may be greenish and hairy, but later get smooth and turn grayish-red. Twigs are marked with raised lenticels and leaf scars. Winter buds are about ¼ inch (6 mm.) long and are covered with about 12 overlapping, hairy bud scales. There is no terminal bud.

The wood is heavy, hard, strong, easy to split and very durable when in contact with the soil. It is used for posts, railroad ties and sills of buildings. It makes good fuel. The inner bark has been used medicinally and for tea.

Note: A commonly planted street tree which closely resembles Slippery Elm is Scotch Elm. It can be distinguished by its nearly black buds, leaves which are often slightly lobed near the tip, and smooth, hairless fruits.

AMERICAN ELM

Ulmus americana L.
Elm Family

American Elm is a large tree 80 to 100 feet in height with a tall, straight trunk terminated by a broad crown of gracefully drooping lateral branches. The trunk often divides into numerous limbs, forming a vase-like frame. This elm grows naturally in rich, moist bottomlands, and is common along streams and bordering lakes and ponds; but because of its graceful beauty, it has been planted in great numbers. This is the tree that is being endangered by the Dutch Elm disease, for which scientists have yet to find a cure.

The simple, alternate, oval-pointed leaves have an *unequal base*. The dark-green leaves are rough, thick, and doubly-toothed at the margins. The primary veins run straight from the midrib to the points of the teeth. The leaves may be from 2 to 6 inches long.

The flowers occur in clusters — each one containing 3 or 4 flowers — on drooping stalks. The flower is perfect (it has both male and female parts) and produces an oval winged fruit (samara) which is borne on a slender stalk. The flat seed is surrounded by a wing which is deeply notched at the bottom and has a fringe of tiny hairs *on the margins* only.

The bark is rather thick, grayish, and roughened by long and irregular furrows separating rather broad, flat ridges. These ridges are occasionally flaky or corky. A cross section of bark will show alternate layers of brown and buff color.

The slender twigs are green and hairy at first, but later become smooth and reddish-brown or grayish-brown. The base of the twigs is often marked with ring-like bud-scale scars.

The buds are alternate, sharp-pointed and covered with from 6-10 overlapping, reddish-brown scales with a darker margin.

The wood is heavy, hard, strong, coarse-grained and hard to split. It is used for plywood, flooring, railroad ties, hoops, and pulp.

CORK or ROCK ELM
Ulmus thomasi (racemosa) Sarg.
Elm Family

Rock Elm is a rather tall tree usually 50-70 feet but it occasionally reaches heights up to 100 feet. It has a straight, slender trunk and slender, stiff, horizontal branches. The lower branches are often strongly drooping.

The oval leaves are similar to those on the American Elm, but have fewer and very straight veins. The base of the leaf is nearly equal, but may be somewhat lop-sided. The leaves are smooth, hairless, on short stalks, and have doubly-toothed margins.

The purplish-yellow flowers are in long, loose, hanging clusters. The long stalked fruit *is hairy all over* — not just over the seed body as on the Slippery Elm. The margin is narrow and it has a pointed tip with a fringe of hairs all around the edge.

The bark is very rough and is perpendicularly deep-furrowed. The twigs are covered with fine hairs and the small branches develop thick, corky ridges. The pointed, hairy buds have scales with dark edges.

The wood is durable, close-grained, heavy, and hard. It was once used for shipbuilding, and is now used for railroad ties, sills of buildings, furniture, and fuel.

1. branchlet with corky ridges
2. winter bud and leaf scars
3. mature fruits

HACKBERRY

Celtis occidentalis L.
Mulberry Family

1. chambered pith
2. winter bud
3. male flower
4. female flower

Hackberry is a small tree usually 30-60 fee tall but occasionally reaching heights up to 80 feet. It has a round-topped crown and a shor trunk. It is not common in New England.

The alternate, simple, narrowly-oval leave have toothed margins, a tapering, slightly curved tip and an inequilateral base. The lea stalks are slender, grooved, and slightly hairy The uppersurface of the leaf is rough.

There may be three kinds of greenish flowers on each tree — male flowers, female flowers, and perfect flowers which contain both male and female reproductive parts. The flowers are on slender, drooping stalks.

The fruits are dark purple berry-like drupe ¼ to ½ inches (8-11 mm.) long with a short thick beak. They are on slender stalks and have a large stone inside.

The gray to brown bark has raised warty projections which are a help in identification Younger branches are dark brown to reddish brown in color. The twigs are slender and zig zag, and may be somewhat hairy or downy The white pith inside is broken into cavities by evenly-spaced, horizontal partitions (chambered). The small buds have 3-4 visible scales with dark margins.

The wood is heavy, not strong, coarse grained and yellowish. It resembles ash. It is not commercially used in New England but would be suitable for fencing, boxes and crates handles, and cheap furniture.

RED MULBERRY
Morus rubra L.
Mulberry Family

Red Mulberry is usually 35-50 feet in height, but occasionally it reaches heights up to 70 feet. The trunk is usually short and subdivides near the ground. The crown is dense, round-topped, and quite spreading. Red Mulberry prefers rich, moist soil of valleys and foothills. It is not commonly found in northern New England.

The alternate leaves are 3-5 inches long with heart-shaped base, toothed margins, and pointed tips. Usually the leaves have three primary veins and are unlobed, but occasionally a tree may have some leaves that are mitten-shaped, with 3, or even 5, lobes. The leaves are rough on the upper surface, downy on the underside, and the veins are sunken in. The leaf scars are almost circular, are concave, and have raised bundle scars.

The male flowers occur in narrow spikes, about 2 inches long, which develop in the axils of the new leaves. The female flowers are in dense spikes about one inch long.

The fruit is juicy, sweet, and edible. It is about an inch (3-6 cm.) long and is composed of many small drupes. It is green at first and turns red and then dark purple when ripe.

The bark begins to roughen about the third year — splitting both longitudinally and diagonally. On older trunks the bark is dark, grayish-brown and peels off in long, narrow flakes.

The stout twigs are smooth, slightly zig zag, greenish-brown tinged with red, and enlarged at the nodes to bear the buds and leaves. A *milky juice is emitted* when the twig is injured. The buds are about 2/5 inch long and are covered with 3-9 greenish bud scales with dark margins. There are no true terminal buds.

The wood is soft, not strong, but is durable when in contact with the soil. It would be good for fence posts, but Red Mulberry is not abundant enough in New England to be of commercial importance.

WHITE MULBERRY
Morus alba L.
Mulberry Family

White Mulberry is very similar to Red Mulberry, so only the distinctive characteristics will be given.

The leaves are *not hairy on the underside —* except possibly some hairy tufts at the axils of the veins. There are apt to be more lobed leaves on the White Mulberry. The leaf base is on a slant with the leaf stem (oblique-based). The fruit is shorter and whitish or paler than that of the Red Mulberry, and is quite tasteless. The buds are red-brown and usually do not have darker scale borders.

This tree was introduced from Europe in an unsuccessful attempt to establish a silkworm industry. It is not common in New England, but cultivated plants have escaped and become naturalized.

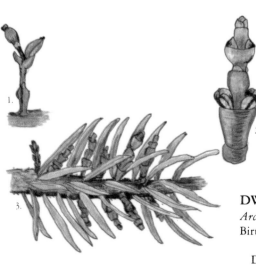

DWARF MISTLETOE
Arceuthobium pusillum Peck
Birthwort Family

Dwarf Mistletoe is a tiny, slightly-woody plant about ½ inch (.6-2 cm.) tall. It is usually parasitic on branches of Black Spruce, but is occasionally found on other conifers. The

1. entire plant in spring (enlarged)
2. entire winter plant greatly enlarged
3. Dwarf Mistletoe growing on Black Spruce

presence of this plant on the spruce often causes "witches' brooms", which are more easily spotted than the mistletoe itself. The stems are smooth and may be olive, purplish or brownish in color. The stems may be simple or branched and are usually brittle at the base. Tiny paired leaves are olive or brown and are pressed close to the stem like scales. These scales are joined together. Tiny flowers appear in the axils of the leaves in the spring. The brown fruit is a tiny, slender, flattened drupe which is usually on a short, curved stalk.

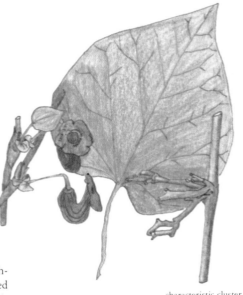

characteristic cluster
of side twigs

DUTCHMAN'S PIPE
Aristolochia durior Hill
Birthwort Family

Dutchman's Pipe is a large, twining or high-climbing shrubby vine with heart-shaped leaves 4-8 inches (.9-2 dm.) long. The shrub is usually hairless. It has been widely planted in the past, and has become naturalized in rich woods and along streams. There is a clasping, leaf-like bract around the stem at the leaf axils. Older branches will have a characteristic cluster of side twigs. The brown-purple flowers are shaped like a pipe. They are about an inch (3 cm.) long and are constricted at the throat and abruptly widen into a three-lobed flat surface. These stalked "pipes" grow from the leaf axils.

JAPANESE KNOTWEED or BAMBOO

Polygonum cuspidatum Sieb. and Zucc.
Buckwheat Family

Japanese Bamboo is *not a shrub*, but because it is tall and bush-like, and some will expect to find it in this book, it has been included.

"Bamboo" is not a bamboo, but a perennial plant 4-8 feet tall which dies back to the ground each winter. The stout, erect stem is rather woody at the base. It is scurfy, dotted, slightly ridged, and much branched. The large leaves are rounded, but abruptly come to a pointed tip. They are on long stalks and have a conspicuous network of veins on both sides. The margins are untoothed, but are usually wavy.

The minute, greenish-white flowers are in lacy, forking clusters. The calyx remains on the stalk when the flowers fall and it becomes broadly winged when in fruit.

The plant is attractive and has been *unwisely planted as an ornamental*, because it rapidly spreads by stout underground shoots and chokes out all nearby vegetation. It is very difficult to eradicate this plant once it has become established. It is found in waste places, neglected gardens, and around old buildings.

VIRGIN'S BOWER

Clematis virginiana L.
Crowfoot Family

Virgin's Bower is a vine which often dies back to the ground, but may winter over and become thick and quite woody. The plants climb by twisting their leaf stalks around nearby shrubs or bushes. Virgin's Bower may be found growing in moist thickets or along streams. The opposite leaves are on long purplish stalks. Each leaf is divided into three coarsely-toothed leaflets. The leaflets vary in size and shape and have a prominent network of veins. The flowers are in loose, leafy clusters. There are no true petals, but there are four creamy-white spreading sepals which look like petals. Numerous white stamens are in a tuft in the center. The fruit is a distinctive cluster of achenes tipped by feathery styles and often called Old Man's Beard. It is similar to that on Purple Clematis (below) but is smaller, and usually there are five or six together in a hairy mass.

PURPLE CLEMATIS

Clematis verticillaris DC.
Crowfoot Family

Purple Clematis is a trailing or partly climbing vine which is somewhat woody — especially at the base. The stem is usually hairless. This vine grows in rocky woodlands and thickets and especially on limy ledges where it climbs to heights of 10 feet or more.

The paired leaves are on long, slender stalks and have three leaflets which are irregularly toothed and pointed. The leaflets have prominent veins which are sunken in on the top surface. The pale lavender to purple-blue flowers are 2-4 inches (5-7.5 cm.) when spread wide, but they usually remain in a rather cupped position. The flowers are solitary on long slender stalks which rise from the leaf axils or at the ends of the branches. There are four thin (nearly translucent) strongly-veined sepals which look like petals. Numerous stamens are in the center. The mature styles split and curl to form a unique fluff ball or nest-like fruit cluster.

COMMON BARBERRY
Berberis vulgaris L.
Barberry Family

enlarged flower

    Common Barberry is an upright shrub with arching branches. It is a native of Europe but has become naturalized in fields and woods throughout New England. It reaches heights of 3-10 feet, has gray bark, and rosettes of paddle-shaped leaves. The margins of the leaves are bristle-toothed. Many of the nodes have a three-pronged thorn and a long cluster of yellow flowers. The fruits are scarlet berries in long, drooping clusters.

JAPANESE BARBERRY
Berberis thunbergii DC.
Barberry Family

    This barberry is usually an escape from cultivation where it has been used a great deal for hedges. It has become naturalized in overgrown pastures, rather open woods, and is quite often found near old dumps. Japanese Barberry is a low, compact oriental shrub with many arching branches.

    The leaves are wedge-shaped and are in small clusters or rosettes containing from 6-10 leaves which are very unequal in size. Below each rosette of leaves is *a single spine.* The leaves turn scarlet in the fall. Leaves on *B. thunbergii* are untoothed while those on *B. vulgaris* are toothed; the spines on *B. thunbergii* are simple while those on *B. vulgaris* are branched, the fruits of *B.*

thunbergii are born singly while those of *B. vulgaris* in long-stalked clusters.

The yellow (sometimes red-tinge on outside) flowers are on long flower stalks. They may occur singly or in groups of from 2-4 and hang below each cluster of leaves.

The fruit is an elongated berry, at first yellow, but becoming bright red. This berry stays on the plant all winter and is relatively unchanged.

The twigs are brown, rather rigid, and branchlets are strongly grooved. The inner bark and wood is yellow.

MOONSEED or YELLOW PARILLA
Menispermum canadense L.
Moonseed Family

Moonseed is a high-climbing vine found in rich thickets and along stream banks. It climbs over other bushes or walls and reaches heights of 6-12 feet.

The margin of the broad leaf is untoothed, but the leaves have from 3-7 shallow lobes. The underside of the leaf is paler in color. The long, slender *leaf stalk is attached inside the edge of the leaf* on the underside. Very tiny flowers are in small whitish to pale green clusters — male and female flowers in separate clusters. The round, berry-like drupe is dark blue with a whitish bloom and looks similar to Frost Grapes. The flattened stone inside is crescent-shaped. Winter buds are one above the other.

1. "moon" seed
2. male flowers
3. female flowers

LAUREL MAGNOLIA or SWEETBAY
Magnolia virginiana L.
Magnolia Family

Laurel Magnolia is a small tree or shrub which is seldom taller than 25 feet in New England, but reaches much greater heights farther south. The trunk is usually short and swollen at the base. It grows in low woods, swamps and other wet places.

The simple, oval, alternate leaves are 3-6 inches (.8-1.5 dm.) long. They have untoothed margins and usually taper at the base to the short stalk. Leaves are evergreen in the south, but will usually fall off in New England. The under surface is covered with a whitish bloom.

The globular, solitary flowers have a calyx and a corolla which are both white but will turn brownish with age. The flower is about two inches long and is very fragrant. It is perfect — containing both male and female reproductive parts. The pistil forms a fleshy and rather woody cone-like red fruit about two inches long. It is composed of many kernel-like carpels — each of which holds one or two berry-like seeds which will hang on a long, thin "thread" when they are mature.

The downy twigs are round, green, and later turn reddish-brown and are roughened by crescent-shaped leaf scars. The pith is solid but is composed of evenly-spaced, alternate, horizontal dark and light-colored layers. Winter buds are silky white. The wood is of no commercial value, but Laurel Magnolia is an extremely attractive natural shrub which is well adapted to planting for ornamental beauty.

TULIP TREE; TULIP POPLAR; YELLOW POPLAR

Liriodendron tulipifera L.
Magnolia Family

branch with cone-like fruit

Tulip Tree is a large, handsome tree of great commercial value. It is uncommon in northern New England, but is found in southern New England. It is usually 50-70 feet high in woodlands, but reaches 190 feet in height. The trunk is usually straight, continuous, and unbranched up to the small, rounded crown. The limbs are slender, mostly horizontal or the lower ones drooping. It grows best in rich, moist soil along streams, on islands, and at the base of mountain slopes.

The long-stalked leaves are smooth and bright yellow-green on top and lighter beneath. The base is rounded and there are usually four untoothed lobes, but the tip comes to an abrupt end as if someone had cut it off. Leaves turn rich russet brown in the fall.

The tulip-shaped flowers have 6 petals arranged in two rows and 3 reflexed sepals. The flower is 3-4 inches (8-10 cm.) across and has pale yellow-green petals which are stained at the base with orange-red. Inside are numerous long, pale-green anthers around the conical pistil. The fruit is light brown, cone-like, and consists of many spirally arranged samaras.

The bark is brownish gray, often with dark or sepia brown, rounded ridges. The perpendicular furrows are deep and short. The smooth, slender twigs are greenish during the first summer, but later become reddish-brown, shiny, and marked by conspicuous pale marks (lenticels). The twigs are also roughened by elevated leaf scars and *rings which encircle the twigs*. The buds are smooth and red-brown, mottled with white dots and covered by a whitish covering. The wood is pale greenish to olive-buff with a whiter sapwood. It is hard, close-grained, straight-grained and easily worked. It is used for interior finish, construction, cabinets, boats, and woodenware.

101

SWAMP or RED BAY
Persea barbonia (L.) Spreng
Laurel Family

Swamp Bay is a small tree which is seldom over 35 feet in height. It grows in swamps and along streams south of New England, but in this area, it has largely been introduced as an ornamental.

The alternate leaves are evergreen and vary from 3-7 inches (7-18 cm.) in length. Young leaves are covered with fine hairs on both sides, but mature leaves become smooth and glossy on top. The leaves are oval or lance-shaped and are narrowed at the base. They are strongly veined and hairy on the underside.

The flowers are perfect (both male and female parts) and are arranged in panicles. Each flower has a hairy calyx with 6 equal or unequal parts. The fruit is a nearly spherical, one-seeded berry. It is from 1/3 to ½ inches (5-12 mm.) long and is dark bluish with a bloom. The berry ripens in September.

The wood is hard, durable, strong, brittle, and close-grained. Farther south where the tree is more plentiful, it is occasionally used for cabinet work or for interior finish, but in New England, Swamp Bay is planted chiefly for ornamental purposes.

male

female

SASSAFRAS
Sassafras albidum (Nutt.) Nees
Laurel Family

Sassafras is a medium-sized tree which may get as tall as 80 feet. It has a stout, rugged, deeply-grooved trunk. The root, branches, flowers, and fruit are all very aromatic when bruised. Sassafras is a tree mostly of upland regions and it prefers rich, sandy loam.

The alternate leaves vary in size and shape. On one branch, one can find unlobed leaves, 2-lobed "mitten" leaves, and leaves with 3 (or rarely 5) lobes. The leaves are very hairy when they first open, but later lose this hair — except at the midrib. Each leaf is on a long leaf stalk.

The male and female flowers are separate — sometimes even on separate trees. The flowers are greenish-yellow, have a calyx with six parts, and are in sprays containing from 10 to 15 individual flowers. The female flower later produces a lustrous blue fruit which is on a fleshy, *club-shaped, red stalk.*

The bark on young saplings is green, spotted with red. Bark of branches is usually reddish brown and very thin, but on older stems, it becomes thick and scaly. Twigs and branches are rather brittle. The buds are alternate, large, sharp-pointed, and have a few loose-fitting, slightly green, bud scales.

The wood is light brown, soft, weak, brittle, very aromatic, and durable when in contact with the soil. The roots and bark are distilled for their oil which is used to perfume toilet articles. The wood is used for posts, rails, furniture, and interior finishes.

1. greatly enlarged leaf bud
2. greatly enlarged flower buds and leaf scar

SPICEBUSH: WILD ALLSPICE: BENJAMIN BUSH

Lindera benzoin (L.) Blume
Laurel Family

Spicebush is a shrub 3-12 feet high with upright stems. It grows in damp woods and at edges of brooks.

The simple, nearly smooth leaves are from 2-5 inches (5-13 cm.) long and taper at the base. The stalked leaves have toothless margins and the widest part of the leaf is above the middle. The leaves are deep green above and are paler and hairless underneath.

Leaf buds are smaller and pointed with 2-3 scales showing. Flower buds are larger and globular. (See inserts.)

Insignificant waxy, golden yellow flowers are in small clusters which are very close to the stem. These appear before the leaves.

The fruit is a short and narrow red, berry-like drupe containing one seed. The fruits grow in small clusters close to the stem. They ripen in July but remain on the bush until fall. The "berry" is aromatic when crushed, as are the twigs. Twigs are smooth, brittle, green or brownish, and are often forked.

A medicine — tincture of benzoin — has been made from this bush.

PRICKLY GOOSEBERRY or DOGBERRY

Ribes cynosbati L.
Gooseberry Family

This gooseberry grows in open loamy or rocky woods. It flowers in May and June and the fruit matures from July to September.

There are slender spines at the axils of the leaves. These spines may be solitary or in groups of 2-3. There may be a few weak prickles on the branches. The leaves are nearly round with coarsely-toothed margins. The base may be rounded or heart-shaped, and the leaf blades are usually covered with soft hairs underneath. The flowers have five small white petals which are inserted in the throat of the calyx. Five stamens alternate with the petals, but *do not protrude* from the center. The flowers are on long stalks and are arranged in small, loose clusters. The *ovary is* usually *covered by glandless prickles*. The large green berry is crowned by shriveled remains of the calyx and may be covered with long, stiff prickles.

SMOOTH-FRUITED WILD GOOSEBERRY
Ribes hirtellum Michx.
Gooseberry Family

This gooseberry grows in rocky woods and swamps to heights of 3-4 feet. The leaves are thin and firm and have 3-5 toothed lobes. The leaves are glandless, but are hairy on the veins on the underside.

The greenish-yellow to dull purple flowers are in small clusters of 1-3. The greenish or purplish sepals are bent backwards and the *stamens are long and protruding*. The ovary is smooth — not hairy or bristly. The fruit is purplish or blackish and *is not hairy*.

The older bark freely peels off in layers. Newer canes are commonly prickly, but fruiting canes usually have no prickles. They may have some spines at the nodes.

enlarged flower — no prickles

EUROPEAN or GOLDEN GOOSEBERRY
Ribes grossularia L.
Gooseberry Family

This gooseberry has spread from cultivation to thickets and roadsides where it reaches heights of 3½ feet. It resembles *R. hirtellum* but the bark on the fruiting canes has no bristles on the middle and upper internodes. Usually there are three stout spines at the nodes, but they may appear singly or in pairs.

Young leaves are hairy. Leaf blades are rounded to heart-shaped at the base and are on short stalks. They have round-toothed lobes. The ovary is covered with soft hairs or is glandular. The flowers are greenish — tinged with pink or red and the stamens are long and easily seen. The fruit may be red, yellow or green with lighter stripes and is usually hairy or has weak bristles.

fruit

BRISTLY BLACK CURRANT
Ribes lacustre (Pers.) Poir.
Gooseberry Family

This shrub reaches heights up to 3 feet and grows in cold woods and swamps. The bruised twigs and berries emit a skunk-like odor.

The young canes and flowering branches are densely covered with bristles. Each flower has five spreading purplish or greenish petals above a *very bristly ovary*. The flowers are in a drooping or spreading cluster of five or more. The leaves are thin, have from 5-7 deeply cut lobes, and are usually hairless. The fruit is purplish-black with gland-tipped bristles. There are slender, weak spines generally clustered at the nodes.

SKUNK CURRANT
Ribes glandulosum Grauer
Gooseberry Family

Skunk Currant is the most common of the currants and gooseberries in our area. The trailing stems are smooth and thornless, and have ascending branches which reach heights up to 2 feet. Most parts of this plant have a strong skunk odor when crushed. This currant grows in cold, wet woods or clearings and on rocky slopes.

The leaves are heart-shaped at the base, are 1-2 inches (2.5-5 cm.) long and have 5 or 7 lobes which are doubly toothed. The leaf stalks are long, slender, and hairless. The blades of the leaves are usually hairless, but some may be slightly hairy along the veins beneath.

The flowers are in small, erect clusters and bloom in May. Each flower has five white (or pinkish) petals in a cup-shaped calyx. The flower stalk, ovaries, and red berries have glandular hairs on them. The bristly red berries are about ¼ inch (6 mm.) in diameter and are in small clusters. The bark of older branches is smooth and has no bristles or prickles. The winter buds are reddish.

RED CURRANT
Ribes triste Pall.
Gooseberry Family

Red Currant is infrequently found in northern and central Maine, New Hampshire and Vermont. It grows in rocky or cool and swampy woods, and may be found in alpine ravines. It is a low reclining or straggling shrub. The rather large leaves are nearly as broad as they are long (up to three inches) and the sides are nearly parallel. The leaf blades have from 3-5 broad, toothed lobes. The leaves have matted whitish "wool" on the underside, but the top surface is smooth. The leaf stalk is reddish. The dull pink, salmon, or purplish flowers are in a drooping cluster on the old wood below the tuft of new leaves. The saucer-shaped calyx is smoky or purplish colored. The small, smooth berries are hard and red. The bark is smooth.

WILD or
AMERICAN BLACK CURRANT
Ribes americanum Mill.
Gooseberry Family

This currant grows in rich woods, moist thickets and along streams. It reaches heights up to 6 feet. The bell-shaped flowers are yellow or whitish and are on downy stalks in drooping clusters of five or more flowers. The stamens do not protrude. The leaves are smooth, but are somewhat hairy and resin-dotted on the underside. The broad leaves are sharply 3-5 lobed with toothed margins and a sharply pointed tip. The fruit is a *shiny, black, hairless berry.* The erect branches have no thorns, but are hairy.

bell-shaped flower

EUROPEAN BLACK CURRANT
Ribes nigrum L.
Gooseberry Family

This currant is very similar to Wild Black Currant, but it has a hairy calyx which is shorter and broader. The flower is greenish-purple or a dull white. The broad leaves are lobed and are resin dotted on the underside only. There are no thorns or bristles. The winter buds are brown and pointed. The berry is smooth and shiny black.

GOLDEN or BUFFALO CURRANT
Ribes odoratum Wendland
Gooseberry Family

This tall shrub has no prickles or thorns. It is common in cultivation, but has escaped and formed roadside thickets in certain localities.

The leaves grow in clusters on long leaf stalks. They are not heart shaped at the base and may have either three or five lobes. There may be teeth on the lobes, or the margins may be untoothed.

The golden-yellow flowers are in small clusters and bloom early before the lilacs. They are very fragrant with a spicy scent. The calyx tube is from 2-3 times as long as the oval, spreading lobes.

The fruit is a black and shiny berry which is very good to eat. It makes good pies.

black berries
not in clusters

enlarged
flower cluster

WITCH HAZEL
Hamamelis virginiana L.
Witch Hazel Family

Witch Hazel is a tall, coarse shrub usually 10 to 12 feet tall, but occasionally growing to a slender, irregular tree 25 feet in height. Quite often there will be from 2-4 short trunks growing in a group. Witch Hazel is common in dry or wet woods, thickets, and open areas.

The rough, dull, deep-olive green leaves are from 2-6 inches (5-15 cm.) long and have *a lopsided base*. The principal veins are rather straight and are very prominent. The leaf margin has coarse, uneven teeth and is somewhat wavy. The leaf surface of young leaves is slightly downy, but mature leaves are smooth. The leaves turn a spotted, dull gold in autumn about the time the flowers begin to open.

The yellow flowers appear in clusters of 2 or 3 in the axils of the leaves. Each has four fertile stamens which alternate with four long, narrow, curling and twisting petals. Blossoms appear in autumn along with the furry, matured woody capsule of the previous season. When this seed capsule splits, it ejects — with great force — four hard, shiny brown seeds which travel for many yards. The flowers may be male only, female only, or perfect.

The bark is sepia or deep-brown blotched with lighter brown and has occasional horizontal markings.

The wood is hard, close-grained, durable, heavy and pale brown. It has no economic value, but an extract for medicine is made from the bark and twigs.

110

SWEET GUM
Liquidambar styraciflua L.
Altingia Family

Sweet Gum is a beautiful tree with a tall, clean trunk and a rounded crown with wide-spreading, horizontal branches. It is commonly 50-70 feet, but reaches heights up to 140 feet. It grows in rich, wet woods from Connecticut southward. It will not tolerate shade.

The simple, alternate leaves are a deep, glossy green color and have a *distinctive star shape*. The hairless leaves may have 5 or 7 toothed, pointed lobes and are fragrant when bruised. The base of the leaf is nearly square and the stalk is long and slender. The leaves turn deep crimson in autumn.

Male flowers are in erect or nodding catkins. Female flowers are in a rounded, long-stemmed head. The fruit is a brown, dry, somewhat prickly, long-stemmed hanging ball about an inch in diameter. The "ball" is made up of many woody capsules which contain tiny winged seeds.

Mature bark is grayish and deep grooves separate the broad, flat, scaly ridges. A sweet, gummy sap is emitted if a twig is broken. Reddish-brown twigs and branches may have *corky wings or ridges*. There are also stubby "spur" branches which are densely covered by leaf scars or crowded buds. The pith is rather large, angular, and very light brown. Reddish-brown conical buds have scales with a hairy fringe, and a rounded back.

The wood is heavy, hard, and close-grained. It takes a high polish and is widely used for fine furniture. The wood is also used for interior finish, boats, toys, boxes, woodenware and fuel.

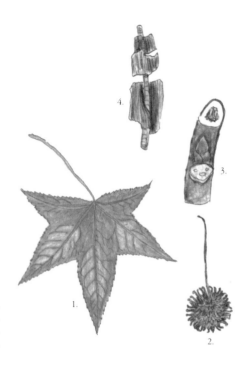

1. leaf
2. a fruit cluster
3. enlarged winter twig with bud and leaf scar
4. branch with corky projections

BUTTONWOOD, PLANETREE
or SYCAMORE
Platanus occidentalis L.
Planetree Family

1.   2.   3.

1. section of a twig with a stipule
2. a head of fruit
3. enlarged winter twig with bud

Buttonwood — our largest deciduous tree — is a massive tree usually 100 feet tall, but occasionally reaching heights more than 150 feet. The trunk usually branches near the base into heavy sub-trunks which re-divide and form a wide-spreading, open irregular crown. It is rare in northern New England — but has survived when planted — and is more common in moist, fertile valleys of southern New England.

The leaves are large — up to 8 inches long — and have 3-5 lobes. The leaves are hairy on the underside and have *long, hollow-based stalks*.

Flowers are small and inconspicuous in dense heads, male and female occurring on separate stalks. The male flowers are dark red and on a stalk in the axils of the upper leaves. Female flowers are greenish, but often tinged with red, and are in long-stalked, drooping clusters. The fruit is a round ball of achenes about one inch in diameter which remains on the tree far into the winter.

The bark is reddish-brown or gray. On older trunks, it breaks off in large, thin plates and exposes the whitish inner bark. The mottled inner bark is characteristic of this tree, but it is usually found on branches high off the ground where it may not readily be seen. The twigs are stout, zig zag, smooth, and brown or gray. They are enlarged at the nodes and are marked with small pale lenticels and encircled by stipule scars (see insert). The pith is white and wide. Some buds are hidden inside the leafstalk of older leaves. The other buds are conical and have three scales — the outer one is smooth and shiny brown, the middle one is green and gummy, and the innermost one is

112

hairy. The buds are surrounded by a distinctive leaf scar. The wood is hard and tough, and is suitable for crates and furniture, but is not common enough in New England to be of commercial importance. It is planted as an ornamental.

NINE-BARK
Physocarpus opulifolius L. Maxim.
Rose Family

Nine-bark is a shrub with recurved branches and peeling bark. It grows in thickets, river-banks, and rocky places to heights of from 3-10 feet. It is often cultivated and occasionally escapes.

The dark green leaves are from 2-4 inches (5-10 cm.) long and are somewhat maple-shaped. They are broad and have three pointed lobes with toothed margins. The base may be heart-shaped, narrowed or rounded.

The flowers are white, but occasionally may be tinged with purple. They grow in rounded, terminal clusters which contain many flowers. Each flower has five rounded petals and twenty or more stamens which are inserted in the throat of the five-lobed calyx. The fruit is a smooth, pink-red inflated pod — usually 3-5 on a stalk — which contains 2-5 round, smooth, yellow shiny seeds with pointed tips.

The old bark on the trunks shreds and sheds into thin strips and layers, but the bark on newer twigs is bright yellow and is not shreddy.

113

enlarged flower

leaf of *S. alba*

MEADOWSWEET
Spiraea latifolia (Ait.) Borkh.
Rose Family

Meadowsweet grows to heights of 2-6 feet in moist or wet places. The alternate leaves may be egg-shaped or broadly lance-shaped and have a coarsely-toothed margin. The small white or pale flesh-colored flowers have five rounded petals with numerous stamens protruding from the center. These flowers are arranged in a pyramidal cluster which is longer than it is wide. There is no odor, even though a fragrance is implied by the name "Meadowsweet."

The twigs are reddish or purplish brown and they are not hairy.

NARROWLEAF MEADOWSWEET or NARROWLEAF SPIRAEA
Spiraea alba Du Roi
Rose Family

This spiraea is similar to Meadowsweet, but has narrow, fine-toothed leaves which are pointed at both ends. The leaves have stalks and are hairy on the veins on the underside. The shrub reaches heights of 2-6 feet and grows in wet or moist soil. The twigs are *yellow-brown and hairy* — especially on young growth. The buds are long-pointed and silky. The white flowers are in long, slender clusters and open from June to September.

STEEPLEBUSH or HARDHACK
Spiraea tomentosa L.
Rose Family

This erect shrub grows in clumps in abandoned pastures and fields to heights up to

hree feet. The oval leaves have unequally-
oothed margins. They are smooth and dark
reen on the upper surface, but are covered
ith a *rusty wool on the underside.* The rose-
ink or purplish flowers grow in elongated
pires at the top of the plant. Each small
lower has five delicate, spreading petals and a
uft of stamens in the center. This tuft gives a
eathery appearance to the pointed flower
pike. When the petals fall, the stiff, tan
lower spike may be dried to be used in dried-
lower arrangements where it is very effective
nd will last for years.

COMMON APPLE
Pyrus malus L.
Rose Family

Apple is not native, but it has spread from
ultivation to fields and woods where it may
emain for many years. In the open it is a low
ree, but in the woods it reaches heights up to
0 feet. The oval leaves are from 1-3 inches
ong, have toothed margins, and rounded or
eart-shaped bases. The undersurface and the
eaf stalks are covered with a white fuzz.
Leaves are often clustered at the tips of short
ew twigs. Winter buds are at the tips of short
ranchlets and are covered with a white fuzz.
The branches on wild trees have short, hard
tems which resemble thorns. Older bark is
ray and flakes off in scales, but bark on new
wigs is green-tan with light-colored lenticels.
This tree is most easily identified by the large
uantity of sour apples it produces after the
inkish-white flowers fall. The fruit is an inch
r more in diameter, but is usually of poor
uality and unsuitable for use.

Needless to say, there are many, many
arieties of this genus.

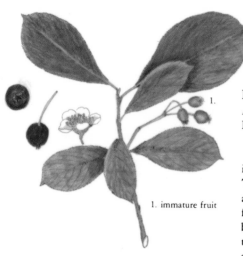

1.

1. immature fruit

PURPLE CHOKEBERRY
Pyrus floribunda Lindl.
Rose Family

Purple Chokeberry is a slender shrub which is usually not more than 10 feet tall (.5-3 m.). The new branchlets, leaves, and flower stalks are all woolly. Purple Chokeberry spreads from underground shoots. It thrives in bogs, but is also found in peat, low wet grounds and thickets, and especially in shaded swamps. The simple, alternate leaves are usually widest above the middle and abruptly come to a pointed tip. The margins have very fine teeth. They are dark blue-green, smooth and rather shiny on the upper surface, but are paler beneath with grayish hairs. Note the glandular hairs on the midrib of the upper surface of the leaf blade. The leaves are variable in size and shape but are usually less than 4 inches (2-9 cm.) in length. The leaves turn shades of pink and old rose in autumn. There are dark glands on the midrib on the uppersurface of the leaf. The flowers are less than ½ inch broad (1 cm.) and have five white or pink-tinged petals. The calyx lobes are longer than they are wide. Usually several flowers are together in a cluster — each on a long hairy stalk. Flowers bloom from April to July. The fruit is a small, nearly round or pear-shaped berry-like pome with the tip creased in to form an indented, five-angled star. When ripe, it is purple or purple-black and juicy and will remain on the tree late into autumn.

This is the same shrub that is listed as *Pyrus arbutifolia* and *Aronia atropurpurea* in other texts.

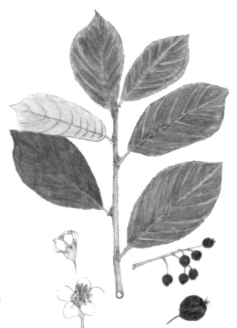

BLACK CHOKEBERRY
Pyrus melanocarpa (Michx.) Willd.
Rose Family

Black Chokeberry is a shrub which is generally from 2-4 feet tall. It grows on rocky uplands, in dry thickets and clearings, or on bluffs and cliffs. A way to distinguish it from Purple Chokeberry is to check for hairiness. There is little or *no hair* on the lower leaf surface, the leaf stalks, or the fruit stalks. A distinguishing characteristic is the *glandular hairs on the midrib* on the uppersurface of the leaf.

The alternate leaves are widest towards the tip and have finely-toothed margins. The margins abruptly taper to a point on most leaves, but on others. there is scarcely any point at all. The underside of the leaf is lighter in color and has a grainy or mealy texture. There is a very narrow, green stipule at the side of each new leaf bud, but this will soon fall off once the leaf opens in the spring.

The white or pinkish flowers have five roundish petals and calyx lobes about as long as they are wide. The flowers are in terminal clusters with smooth flower stalks.

The fruit is a black or very dark purple, juicy pome about ¼ inch (7-10 mm.) in diameter which is similar to a huckleberry. The stems are grayish brown with white fuzz on newer twigs. Reddish leaf buds form in late summer.

AMERICAN MOUNTAIN ASH

Pyrus americana (Marsh.) DC. or
  Sorbus americana Marsh.
Rose Family

American Mountain Ash is a small ornamental tree usually 15-20 feet tall, but occasionally reaches heights to 30 feet in favorable places. It may be reduced to a shrub at higher elevations. It grows naturally in cool mountain woods, on riverbanks, and is common on mountain slopes.

The alternate, compound leaves have from 13-15 elliptical leaflets which taper to a point and have sharply double-toothed margins. The leaf stalks are bright red, and the leaflets are bright green on top and a paler color underneath. Elders have similar compound leaves, but they are opposite while leaves on American Mountain Ash *are alternate.*

The small, white flowers are in broad flat-topped clusters. Each flower has five rounded petals and many stamens. The flowers usually open in May and June. The fruit is bright, shining, coral red and is arranged in crowded clusters about five inches broad — spreading on *dark red stems.* They ripen in late August and September, have a very acid taste, but are relished by the birds.

The bark is neutral or brownish-gray with the smooth surface irregularly broken with plate-like scales. The twigs are pale brown, smooth, but containing conspicuous, scattered, gray dots. Winter buds are sticky. The wood has no economic value, but the tree is planted for its ornamental value and as a food for wild birds.

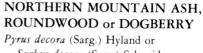

NORTHERN MOUNTAIN ASH, ROUNDWOOD or DOGBERRY

Pyrus decora (Sarg.) Hyland or
  Sorbus decora (Sarg.) Schneid
Rose Family

This mountain ash closely resembles *P. americana* but when well-developed mature plants are available, the two can be distinguished by the leaves. The leaflets of this species are shorter and have more rounded tips, and are blue-green above and whitish beneath. The tree itself is more rounded and more handsome than *P. americana*. The fruits are twice as large on this mountain ash, and the inner bud scales have long silky hairs. The habitats are similar, but the range of *P. decora* is slightly more northern.

EUROPEAN MOUNTAIN ASH

Pyrus aucuparia (L.) Gaertn or
  Sorbus aucuparia L.
Rose Family

This mountain ash is similar to American Mountain Ash, but the leaflets are *not taper pointed*. A hand lens will show white hairiness on the underside of the leaflets. The teeth on the margins are *not on the bottom third* of the leaflet.

The flower cluster is not as flat-topped as the preceding mountain ash, and it is formed earlier. The bright, scarlet fruit is in rounded clusters. The fruit is much larger in *P. aucuparia* than in *P. americana* or *P. decora*. Winter buds are hairy and *are not* sticky.

This mountain ash is planted chiefly as an ornamental and it does not often escape to become established.

SHADBUSH

Amelanchier Spp.
Rose Family

There are many closely related species of Shadbushes in New England. They are called Shad, Service-berry, Sarvice-berry, Juneberry, and Sugar Plum. Some of these can be identified by amateurs, but others are separated only by technical differences which are not in the scope of this book.

The following characteristics generally hold true of all *Amelanchier* shrubs and will help beginners to identify them as "one of the Shadbushes". For further identification, one must consult a botanical manual.

Leaves: round or oval with fine teeth on the margins. The leaves are simple and have stalks.

Flowers: clusters of white flowers with five linear petals and a tuft of stamens in the center. These bloom before the leaves are developed fully.

Fruit: a sweet, round, berry-like pome with many small seeds. The "berry" is on a long stalk and is edible.

Buds: usually reddish

Shadbushes are shrubs or small trees which grow in a clump.

ROUND-LEAVED SHADBUSH
Amelanchier sanguinea (Pursh) DC.
Rose Family

Round-Leaved Shad grows on non-limy ledges, gravelly banks of streams, rocky slopes or ocean shores, but it is not as common as many other shads. This shad is a low straggling or arching shrub 3-10 feet in height. Usually there will be a single, slender trunk, but sometimes there will be two or three together. The *branchlets are red* or reddish, and the winter buds are slender, red-brown, and are not shiny. The leaves are all — or nearly so — unfolded at flowering time. Young leaves have pale hairs beneath, but at maturity, the hair is only on the leaf stalk and the midrib on the underside. The mature leaf blade is oblong to nearly round with a blunt tip and a round or nearly heart-shaped base. Leaves may be 1-2 inches in length and are coarsely-toothed all the way to the base. There are usually 12 to 15 pairs of primary veins and the upper veins are straight and run directly to the point of a tooth. The ovary in the flower of the young fruit is hairy on the tip. Mature fruit is dark purple and juicy. This shad may cross with other shads and make identification very difficult for all but a trained botanist.

Amelanchier wiegandii Nielsen
Rose Family

This *Amelanchier* grows on rocky ledges, banks of streams, and in sand and is similar to *A. laevis*, but has shorter winter buds. It is rare in New Hampshire, found in Maine and Vermont, and is not found in southern New England except in a few places along the Connecticut River. The leaves are bronze to purple and are fuzzy as they expand. The teeth on new leaves are thin and almost wire-like. Leaves get larger after the flowers fade, and mature leaves are 1¼ to 2⅜ inches (3-6 cm.) long. The blade abruptly comes to a short point. Usually there are from 9-11 pairs of main veins which fork at the tips. By autumn, leaves are smooth and have lost all fuzziness. The petals of the flowers are linear with the broadest part of the petal above the middle. The sepals are sharply turned downward at flowering time. Winter buds are up to ⅜ inch (1 cm.) long.

Amelanchier humilis Wieg.
(not shown)
Rose Family

Amelanchier humilis is a rare shrub of north-western Vermont, which grows in loose colonies and spreads by means of underground stolons or suckers. Colonies are 1-25 feet (.3-8 m.) in height and grow on rocky or sandy shores and banks. This *Amelanchier* hybridizes with other *Amelanchiers*, varies greatly, and has several varieties listed which make identification almost impossible for most people.

The leaves are partly or fully expanded at flowering time. Young leaves have white or gray hair on the lower surface, but usually become smooth at maturity. Leaves are 1-2 inches (2.5-5 cm.) long and ¾-1 inch (2-4 cm.) wide, are broad with a rounded tip, and have a heart-shaped base. Margins may have coarse teeth or be untoothed. There are 7-13 pairs of primary veins which fork at the end and enter the teeth. The erect flower clusters have silky hairs on the stalks. The round fruit is black with a bloom, juicy, and sweet.

Amelanchier gaspensis (Wieg.) Fern & Weath.

Rose Family

Amelanchier gaspensis is occasionally found in Maine in eastern Aroostook County but is not found elsewhere in new England. It grows on cliffs, ledges, and shores and is rarely taller than three feet (1 m.) in height. This *Amelanchier* is similar to *A. sanguinea* but the veins do not enter the teeth of the leaf. Expanding leaves are not hairy on top, but may be slightly hairy on the lower surface. Mature blades are thin, broadly-elliptic and abruptly end in a broad, almost flat tip. Margins are not toothed all the way to the base, and there are 6-13 pairs of primary veins. The flower clusters are loose and open with nearly hairless stalks. There are large leaves at the base of the lower few flower stalks. Petals are narrow and the sepals are long but *do not bend downward*. The fruit is ⅜ inch (1cm.) in diameter and is smooth, nearly black, juicy, and sweet.

WOOLLY SHADBUSH

Amelanchier stolonifera Wieg.

Rose Family

This shad grows in dry, sterile, rocky or sandy open places. It is often found along river banks on the coastal plain, but also ascends to summits of mountains.

The expanding leaves are only half grown at flowering time. They have *whitish hairs on the underside*. Mature leaf blades are dull green above and are oblong to somewhat circular with a slight point. The margins are coarsely and sharply toothed, but only along the *upper two-thirds of the margin*. The upcurved primary veins are mostly in pairs — usually 7-9 pairs. Winter buds are dull reddish brown.

Woolly Shadbush produces underground stolons and the plants occur in loose colonies.

CANADA SHADBUSH
Amelanchier canadensis (L.) Medic
Rose Family

winter bud
and leaf scar

This shad usually is less than 20 feet high and has several upright trunks forming a clump. It is common in northern New England and grows on hillsides, in moist thickets, and in open woodlands. Young leaves are covered with woolly hairs and are often in a folded position. They have finely and evenly toothed margins and rounded or slightly-heart-shaped bases. Mature leaves may be elliptical or be broadest above the middle with a rather broad point. The fruit is purple-black with a whitish covering when ripe. The bark on mature trees is gray, variegated with sepia brown stripes. Winter buds are long, slender, and pointed and are covered by bud scales which have hairy margins.

Amelanchier intermedia Spach
(not shown)
Rose Family

Amelanchier intermedia is rare, and in New England is only found in the northern part. It grows in swamps, bogs, thickets and on shores. It is similar to *A. canadensis*, but the full grown leaves are often purplish and the young leaves have only sparse hair — or none at all — while those on *A. canadensis* are heavily white-felted on the under surface. Mature leaf blades are heart-shaped and are 1-2½ inches (2.5-6 cm.) long and ¾ to 1¼ inches (1.8-3 cm.) broad. The tip usually has a short point. The flower cluster is open and the stalks and calyx are nearly hairless.

enlarged
terminal bud

DOWNY SERVICEBERRY
Amelanchier arborea (Michx. F.) Fern.
Rose Family

    This is one of the taller *Amelanchiers* — often growing to heights of nearly 60 feet. It is similar to *Amelanchier laevis*, but the young leaves are covered with *soft woolly hairs that disappear* as the leaves mature. This shad grows in rich woods, thickets, and on slopes.

    The leaves are from 2-4 inches long, have 11-17 pairs of primary veins, and are sharply or doubly-toothed at the margins.

    The flowers are usually white, but occasionally are a rosey pink. They blossom before the leaves unfold. The five linear petals are limber and reflexed.

    The fruit is reddish purple, and is dry and tasteless. The winter buds are long, slender, and pointed. The bud scales are sometimes twisted and the bud may have a pinkish or greenish tinge.

EARLY or SMOOTH-LEAVED SHADBUSH
Amelanchier laevis Wieg.
Rose Family

    This shad is usually less than thirty feet tall. The flower clusters are looser than those on some other shads and the new foliage is bronze or purple tinged at flowering time. This shad is common throughout New England and grows on damp wooded banks, near swamps or clearings, and in thickets.

    The leaves are distinctly elliptical and come to a point more abruptly than does the leaf of *A. canadensis*. The leaf blade is dark green on top, paler underneath, but *is not hairy*. The leaf is up to 3 inches long and may have a heart-shaped or rounded base. The broadest part of the leaf is at or below the middle. The teeth are almost awl-shaped with rounded indentations (sinuses) between. There are from 12-17 pairs of primary veins.

MOUNTAIN or BOG SHADBUSH
Amelanchier bartramiana (Tausch) Roemer
Rose Family

Mountain Shadbush can be distinguished from other shads by its habitat and its small clusters of flowers or fruits. This shrub is from 2-9 feet tall and grows in bogs, wet thickets, or on mountain slopes. It is not too common. It is the only shad found at elevations above 2500 feet. The plant is usually hairless — except for the early bracts which soon fall off. The leaves are smooth, thin and pliable, and dull green in color. They are elliptical with the tip and the base being nearly equal in size. Though alternate, the leaves are sometimes bunched together at the tips of the new growth. The leaf stalk is short and may have silky hairs. The margins are closely toothed nearly to the base of the leaf blade. The flowers are in small clusters of from 1-4. One flower is terminal and the others in the cluster arise from leaf axils. Each flower is on a long, slender stalk and has five petals which are broadest at the middle. Many times, only one fruit will form from each flower cluster. The berry-like pome may be oval or pear-shaped and has five triangular sepals at the tip. When ripe, it is purple with a bloom. The seeds inside are curved.

HAWTHORN or HAW
Crataegus Spp.
Rose Family

There are many species of Hawthorns or Haws in our area. Most are thorny shrubs or small trees with crooked, twisted, and rather interwoven branches. The apple-blossom-like pink or white flowers are in clusters and bloom early in the spring. In autumn, tiny apple-like fruits mature. Different species have different colored fruits, but they are usually red, yellow, orange or a combination of these colors.

Hawthorns are a difficult group for beginners to identify. Some very technical characteristics separate one from another. Some hawthorns are given here as examples, but probably most people using this book will have to be content to identify their specimen as "one of the hawthorns" unless he can enlist the aid of an expert.

HAWTHORN; LANGE'S THORN; BILTMORE HAW
Crataegus biltmoreana Beadle
Rose Family

This hawthorn is an irregularly-branched shrub or occasionally a small tree up to 15 feet in height. It grows in dry, rocky woods and hillsides from Vermont southward. *It does not have as many spines* as most hawthorns have, but instead *has gland-tipped hairs* on the leaf stalks, flower stalks, twigs, and bases of the leaves.

The leaves are broadly oval in general outline but have sharply-toothed margins — the lower teeth at the base have glands on the tips. Usually the leaves have 3-5 pairs of small, triangular-shaped lobes. The leaves and leaf stalks are very hairy.

Usually there are 3-7 flowers in a hairy cluster. About 10 white or pale yellow stamens are in the center. The calyx lobes below the flower have hair-tipped teeth.

The fruit is dull orange or reddish and is somewhat globular in shape. It is hairy — at least when young — and has thin, dry flesh with 3-5 nutlets inside.

COCKSPUR THORN
Crataegus crus-galli L.
Rose Family

Cockspur Thorn is a small tree up to 25 feet in height with a short trunk and stout, spreading branches which form a broad, flat crown. It commonly grows in sandy and dry gravelly soil in thickets and open ground.

The alternate, simple, eliptical leaves may have the *widest part above the middle.* The tip is somewhat rounded or may have an abrupt, short point. The margins are *sharply-toothed, except towards the tapering base.* Mature leaves are thick, smooth, shiny dark green on the top surface and may be 1-4 inches long.

Saucer-shaped flowers appear in June when leaves are fully developed. They contain both female and male parts, are white, and are arranged in small clusters called corymbs. Each flower has about 10 pink- or yellow-tipped stamens in the center.

The fruit ripens in September, but lasts into the winter. It is a short, oblong fruit which may be five-angled. It is greenish to dull red and has 2 small, grooved nutlets inside. The flesh is hard and dry.

The bark is grayish to reddish-brown and is sometimes roughened by small scales. The twigs are smooth, greenish, and slender at first, but later turn light brown or gray. The twigs have straight or slightly curved unbranched, brown thorns 3-4 inches long. The globular buds are at the base of the thorns. The buds are covered with numerous, blunt-pointed scales.

DOTTED HAW or
DOTTED HAWTHORN

Crataegus punctata var. *aurea* Jacq. Ait.
Rose Family

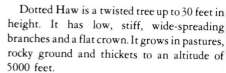

Dotted Haw is a twisted tree up to 30 feet in height. It has low, stiff, wide-spreading branches and a flat crown. It grows in pastures, rocky ground and thickets to an altitude of 5000 feet.

The leaves are a dull, grayish-green and may be smooth or slightly downy along the veins underneath. They are usually 2-3 inches long, have a wedge-shaped base, and the *broadest part is toward the tip.* The veins are very prominent on the top. The margins are coarsely toothed and some leaves may be somewhat lobed towards the tip.

Several white apple blossom-like flowers occur together in a loose cluster. Each is almost ¾ of an inch broad and has five petals and 20 red or yellow-tipped stamens. The fruit is an ocher or orange, *yellow dotted*, berry-like pome which has 3-5 nutlets inside.

The bark is brownish-gray and grooved on the trunk. The twigs have slightly-curved thorns 1-2 (usually 1½) inches long.

The drawing given is for the variety *aurea* because of the golden yellow fruits. There are several other varieties which vary slightly.

ROUND-LEAVED THORN

Crataegus chrysocarpa Ashe
Rose Family

This hawthorn is similar to the preceding ones but it *has very thorny branchlets.* It is a round-topped shrub or occasionally a small tree reaching heights up to 20 feet. It grows in thickets and on rocky ground along streams.

The leaves are broad and roundish with coarsely-toothed margins with 3-4 pairs of triangular lobes. They are a dark, shiny, yellow-green above and may be slightly hairy below. The saucer-shaped flowers have from 5-10 (usually 10) white or pale yellow-tipped stamens. The *calyx lobes on this hawthorn are toothed*. The fruit is dark red or sometimes yellow-gold. It has soft flesh, reflexed calyx-lobes at the tip, and 3-4 nutlets inside.

Crataegus faxoni Sarg.
(not shown)
Rose Family

This *Crataegus* grows in rocky pastures and borders of woods where it reaches heights of 12-15 feet (3-4 m.). It has numerous stems and slender, thorny branches which have long, soft hairs when young. The oval-pointed or elliptic leaves have sharply-toothed margins. Immature blades are coated with short, appressed hairs on the top surface and are densely covered with pale hairs on the under surface. Mature leaves are nearly hairless. The flowers are ½ to 1½ inches (1-1.4 cm.) wide and only a few are in each compact cluster. *Flower stalks are densely hairy.* There are 5-10 stamens with pale yellow anthers. The fruit is oblong or nearly round, is less than ½ inch (.8-1 cm.) in diameter, and has thin, dry flesh with 3 or 4 nutlets inside. *C. faxoni* has been recorded in New Hampshire and probably occurs elsewhere in northern New England, but because most *Crataegus* are difficult to identify, it may have been overlooked.

Crataegus jonesae Sarg.
(not shown)
Rose Family

This *Crataegus* is frequently found on borders of streams and rocky banks along the coast of Maine, but it is rarely — if ever — found elsewhere in New England. *C. jonesae* is tree-like with branches which curve alternately in opposite directions. The thorny branchlets are very hairy when young. It resembles *C. chrysocurpa*, but the leaves are more narrowed — especially at the base. The thick, veiny leaves remain hairy on the underside throughout the season. There are many flowers in the loose, hairy clusters. Each flower is ¾-1 inch (2-2.3 cm.) wide, and has 10 stamens with *large pink anthers*. The sepals are long and untoothed. The oblong fruit is thick, bright red, and has thick, mealy flesh with 2-3 (usually 3) nutlets inside.

Crataegus brainerdi Sarg.
(not shown)
Rose Family

Cratyaegus brainerdi grows in thickets and pastures, and may be a shrub which flowers when only 6-9 feet (2-3 m.) or it may reach heights of 18-25 feet (6-7 m.). When tree-height, it usually has slender, straight, or alternately-curving, thorny branches. The leaves are sharply-toothed and usually have 4-6 pairs of small, pointed lobes. Young leaves may have a few short hairs, but mature leaves

are thin, firm, hairless, and blue-green in color. Flowers are about ¾ inch (1.6-1.8 cm.) wide and there are usually from 4-12 in a cluster. The flower *stalks are not hairy*. Each flower has about *20 stamens* with pink anthers. The oblong fruit has thick flesh with 2-5 (usually 3) nutlets inside.

Crataegus macrosperma Ashe
(not shown)
Rose Family

Crataegus marcrosperma grows in rocky woods and thickets and usually reaches tree height of 18-25 feet (6.7 m.) but may be shorter and more shrub-like. The trunk and larger branches are often angled or buttressed, and are covered with pale, scaly bark. The oval-pointed leaves have sharp teeth on the margin and *five pairs of broad, triangular lateral lobes*. Young leaves may have short hairs on the upper surface, but mature leaves are thin and hairless. The leaf stalks are slender, ⅝ to 1¼ inches (1.5-3 cm.) long and may be glandular. Usually there are 5-12 flowers in each cluster. Flower *stalks are not hairy*. Each flower is more than ½ inch (1.3-1.7 cm.) and has 10 (or fewer) stamens with *red anthers*. The bright red fruit has thick, succulent flesh with 3-5 nutlets inside.

*This *species is variable* and has many varieties and forms. This makes exact identification impossible for all but the experts. For further help, refer to *Gray's Manual of Botany*.

FROSTED HAWTHORN
Crataegus pruinosa (Wendl.) K. Koch
Rose Family

This hawthorn is usually a small tree about 20 feet tall which grows in thickets and on rocky ground. The leaves are smooth, bluish-green, and are *broadest below the middle*. At maturity, they are 1-1½ inches long and have a rounded to abruptly-narrowed base. The margins may be deeply toothed or have 3-4 pairs of shallow, toothed lobes. There are only a few flowers (5-10) in each cluster. The saucer-shaped flowers have 5 petals and 20 pink-tipped stamens. The dark, purple red or dull crimson fruit has prominent sepals at the tip, and is covered with small dots. The *fruit is often slightly angled.* The slender spines are 1-2½ inches long.

SCARLET HAWTHORN
Crataegus pedicellata Sarg.
Rose Family

This hawthorn is occasionally found in southern New Hampshire and Vermont, and is more common in southern New England. It is a tall shrub or a low tree top to 25 feet in height. It grows in thickets and along banks of streams. There are usually many flowers in each cluster. The flowers have 10-20 pink-tipped stamens. The leaves have a rather wide base and are just a *little longer than they are wide.* The margin is sharply-toothed nearly to the base and may have 4-5 pairs of pointed, toothed lobes. Mature leaves are firm, thick, and bluish-green. The fruit has five sepals at the top which may stand erect or spread flat. The *oval, bright red fruit* has dark dots on it and it may be smooth or slightly hairy. The bark is dark gray and scaly. The spines are 1-2 inches long.

Crataegus submollis Sarg.
(not shown)
Rose Family

    Crataegus submollis is usually a tree reaching heights up to 35 feet (8-10 m.) but may be more shrub-like with arching branchlets. The bark is brownish-gray and is slightly scaly. This *Crataegus* grows on wooded hillsides and open fertile ground. The coarsely-toothed, dark green leaves are egg-shaped with 4-5 pairs of shallow lateral lobes. There are many flowers in each loose cluster. Each flower is nearly an inch (2-2.2 cm.) wide and has 10 (or fewer) stamens with *white or pale yellow anthers*. Both the leaves and flower stalks are densely hairy at flowering time. The fruit is bright red, slightly hairy at the ends, has mellow flesh with 5 nutlets inside, and has prominent sepals at the tip.

SHRUBBY CINQUEFOIL
Potentilla fruticosa L.
Rose Family

    This cinquefoil is also called Five Finger or Golden Hardhack, but the name given above is most common. It grows in wet or dry open ground in meadows or along shores to a height of from one to three feet. It is a shrubby plant with erect, branching stems, many divided leaves, and bright yellow flowers. The stems are woody — especially at the base — and have loose bark peeling off in shreds. The leaves are divided into from five to seven narrow leaflets with *toothless margins*. The olive, yellow-green leaves are silky or woolly with white hairs on the undersides, and the edges of the leaves sometimes curl backwards. The flowers are generally an inch or more broad and have five rounded, spreading petals.

THREE-TOOTHED CINQUEFOIL

Potentilla tridentata Ait.
Rose Family

Three-Toothed Cinquefoil is a tiny plant with a woody base which grows at higher elevations — especially on dry, rocky slopes. Sometimes it forms great patches on soil-covered rocks, but it also grows in the cracks of ledges on mountains where there is no appreciable amount of soil. The leaves are clustered near the base of the plant. Each leaf is divided into three leaflets, each of which will be notched or have three teeth at the tip. The leaves turn deep red in the fall. The slender flower stalk rises above the leaf cluster and divides near the tip to hold several stalked flowers in a very loose-spreading cluster. Below the point where the branching occurs are several long thin bracts. Each blossom has five spreading white petals and many long yellow stamens. The entire plant is rarely taller than five inches and is much smaller where soil is poor.

enlarged flowers

BLACKBERRY, BRAMBLE, RASPBERRY or DEWBERRY

Rubus Spp.
Rose Family

There are over two hundred species of brambles in our area. Most of the plants have woody, prickly stems and leaves which are divided into pointed leaflets with toothed margins. Because of the complexity of this genus only seven species will be given. A typical red raspberry, black raspberry, low-running dewberry, smooth blackberry, and highbush blackberry will be included as samples, and the person needing more specific identification should consult more scientific volumes such as *Gray's Manual of Botany* by looking up the genus *Rubus*.

PURPLE-FLOWERING RASPBERRY
Rubus odoratus L.
Rose Family

This erect and branching shrub grows in rocky woods or moist ravines to heights of from 3-5 feet. It has maple-shaped leaves which are from 5-10 inches broad. The leaves and the stem are both rather hairy, but *not prickly* like other raspberries. On older, larger stems, the bark sheds. The broad, five-petaled flower is similar to that of a rose. It may be pinkish to purplish and up to 2 inches across. It has broad, long, brown sepals. After the flower fades, a rather flat raspberry forms. When it is ripe, it is edible, but is rather sour and dry.

RED RASPBERRY
Rubus idaeus L.
Rose Family

Red Raspberry has upright canes from 3-6 feet in height which rise from underground suckers and stolons. It usually grows in dry or rocky places. The tips of the canes do not take root as they do on some other members of this genus. The canes may be prickly, bristly, or nearly smooth, but are usually covered with weak, glandular bristles.

The leaves have 3-5 (occasionally 7) pointed leaflets which do not originate from one point on the central stalk (pinnately arranged) as is the case on *R. allegheniensis*. The side leaflets are not stalked. The leaflets have toothed margins and are white or gray on the underside. The flowers are in small, drooping clusters. The calyx is often bristly or velvety, and the pointed sepals about equal the narrow white petals. The red fruit is usually rather round or flattened, but it may be slightly elongated. Note the *white projection which is left* on the stalk after the edible fruit is removed. There are many varieties of this species in our area, but the one shown is typical.

BLACK RASPBERRY
Rubus occidentalis L.
Rose Family

Black Raspberry has canes which are *heavily whitened with a bloom*. The canes may be *armed with hooked prickles,* but it is not bristly. The canes are long-arching — up to 10 or 12 feet in length — and often take root at the tips. This raspberry grows in rich thickets, ravines, and at the borders of woods.

The leaves usually have three leaflets, which are white beneath. When there are five leaflets, then they are arranged palmately (all from one point on the stalk) and the upper side leaflets and the end leaflets are stalked. The margins of the leaflets are doubly-toothed.

The flowers are in small, terminal clusters. The calyx on the fruit may be somewhat hairy, but it is rarely ever bristly. The sepals are much longer than the small white petals on the flower. The edible fruit is purple black, and usually round rather than elongated. The white core remains on the receptacle when it is picked, leaving a hole at the base of the "berry".

137

LOW-RUNNING BLACKBERRY
Rubus flagellaris Willd.
Rose Family

This blackberry has horizontal stems which trail on or near the surface of the ground to a length of several feet. The stems are not bristly, but on some plants the stems have curved spines. The branches grow upright from the creeping stems to a height of from four to twelve inches and are often prickly or hairy. The leaves are divided into from three to seven thin leaflets, but the most common is three. The sharply toothed leaflets have points at the tips but are rounded at the base. The white flowers are nearly one inch across and have five petals, which are slightly longer than the five green sepals. Numerous stamens in the center of the flower give it a tufted, fuzzy appearance. The fruit is a black "berry" which is very tasty, but has large seeds. The "berry" varies in size from one-half to one inch long.

SWAMP DEWBERRY

Rubus hispidus L.
Rose Family

Swamp Dewberry is a trailing vine with woody, bristly canes. It grows in moist or dry, open soil, in ditches, swales and open woods. The semi-evergreen leaves are lustrous dark green — often with purplish or bronze-tinged under surfaces. The leaves usually have three (rarely five) short-pointed, blunt-toothed leaflets. The leaf stalks have bristles. The small white flowers are in a lax cluster. The flower stalks and the calyx are hairy. The seedy fruit is purple, but blackens with age. It is edible, but is not especially palatable.

SMOOTH BLACKBERRY

Rubus canadensis L.
(not shown)
Rose Family

Smooth Blackberry is quite similar to Highbush Blackberry, which follows. The canes are upright or arching and up to 10 feet in length. The wand-like canes are usually unarmed, but sometimes have a few weak prickles. This blackberry grows in thickets and clearings.

The leaves are very similar to those on Highbush Blackberry. The stalks are long and hairless, and the thin, oval *leaflets are not velvety underneath*. The flowers are similar to those on Highbush Blackberry but the flower stalks are hairless. The fruit is sweet and black when ripe and is quite juicy or pulpy. The big difference between the two blackberries shown is the amount of hairiness. This one lacks hair while the following species does not.

HIGHBUSH BLACKBERRY
Rubus alleghaniensis Porter
Rose Family

The Highbush Blackberry has erect or high-arching canes which reach heights up to 10 feet. The canes may have scattered prickles or may be practically smooth. This is a very confusing species and there are many varieties in our area. The one shown is typical of the highbush blackberries.

The leaves are green on both sides and have from 3-7 leaflets. Usually there are five leaflets which are palmately arranged (the base of each leaflet originates at the same point on the main stalk). The leaf stalks may be armed with prickles on some varieties. The leaves are densely covered with woolly hairs on the underside; they are velvety to the touch. The terminal leaflet may be heart-shaped or broadly-rounded at the base, and is on a short stalk which originates where the side leaflets are attached to the main stalk.

The black, shiny, edible fruit is round or thimble-shaped and may either be fleshy and favorful or rather dry. The fruit *does not separate from the receptacle and leave a projection* above the sepals as does the fruit on the raspberry. The base of the fruit does not have a hole, but the core remains inside the "berry" when it is picked.

MULTIFLORA ROSE
Rosa multiflora Thunb.
Rose Family

   This rambling rose has a trailing or arching habit. It was formerly cultivated and has now escaped to roadsides and moist thickets or borders of woods. The leaves usually have 7 or 9 oval, toothed leaflets in pairs on a central midrib. The destinctive characteristic of this rose is the *deeply-fringed stipules* at the base of each leaf.

   There are numerous white flowers in a pyramidal cluster. Each flower is ¾ to 1½ inches (2-4 cm.) wide. The many pistils form a protruding column in the center of the flower. The fruit is a typical rose hip, but it is hairless and the sepals are not present at the tip of the fruit.

SWEETBRIER
Rosa eglanteria L.
Rose Family

   A distinguishing feature of this plant is the stout prickles which curve downward. The long arching stems have many pink flowers which are smaller than most other roses. The leaflets are more round than those of most roses and are double toothed — there is a smaller tooth between each two larger teeth.

141

BRISTLY or NORTHEASTERN ROSE
Rosa nitida Willd.
Rose Family

This low, slender shrub is found in swamps bogs, or moist soil. It grows to a height of from one to three feet. The stem has many slender straight, dark purple prickles which are all about the same length. The fine prickles extend into the flower cluster. The flower is pink and about two inches broad. The leaf has many small crowded leaflets.

COMMON WILD ROSE, LOW or PASTURE ROSE
Rosa virginiana Mill.
Rose Family

This rose is a low or bushy rose with either dull or shiny green compound leaves with from 3-9 (but usually 5) thin, toothed leaflets The teeth are only on the upper three-fourths of the leaflet. The appendages at the base of the leaf stalk (stipules) are narrow and flare out at the tips. Identifying features of this rose are the glandular hairs which are on the round fruit, the stems and the sepals. The upper half of the canes are armed with slender nearly-straight prickles which are wide at the base The stems are ruddy-brown color, and the canes are very bristly — especially at the lower part of the plant.

The pale pink or deep crimson flowers are 2-3 inches broad and usually fade in color after opening. The roses may be single or in small clusters. The long, pointed sepals are reflexed when the flower is blooming, but spread wide as the fruit matures. When the fruit is bright red, these sepals fall off. The globular berry-like fruit is covered with glandular hairs.

This rose grows to heights up to six feet and grows in dry or rocky soil or in moist to dry thickets, clearings, and in swamps.

SWAMP ROSE
Rosa palustris Marsh.
Rose Family

trough-like stipules

Swamp Rose closely resembles *R. virginiana* but is less common. It usually grows in swamps or wet thickets and shores, and can be distinguished from *R. virginiana* by the *firm narrow stipules* with their parallel sides which fold over and form a trough. Stipules on the Common Rose are broader and more leaflike. The upper branches are smooth, except for a *pair of hooked prickles at the nodes*. The base of the older canes bear stout, hard, pale-colored conical prickles. Each leaf has from 5-9 dull green leaflets which are pointed at both the tip and the base. The margins of the leaflets are minutely toothed nearly to the base and the underside of the leaflets has minute hairs. The flowers may be single or in a flat-topped cluster. The calyx tube is cup-shaped and has glandular hairs on it. It blooms until late August in northern New England, but earlier farther south. This rose reaches heights of from 2-8 feet.

PASTURE ROSE
Rosa carolina L.
Rose Family

straight prickle
at leaf node

This rose grows in dry sandy, rocky or open places or in thin woods. It is a low, slender shrub which is usually less than three feet in height. The canes are usually single and rise from stolons. These canes are thick at the base and may have a few scattered prickles. A distinctive characteristic is the horizontal, straight prickle which grows only where the leaves branch off from the main stem. The middle and upper nodes may not have prickles. The leaves have from 5-9 small, narrow, paired leaflets with toothed margins. The leaves are dull green in color and are downy on the underside. The flowers are usually solitary. The calyx may be smooth or glandular. The round, red fruit is bristly. The stems are slender — often red — and are armed with straight or slightly recurved prickles.

RUGOSA, SEASIDE, or WRINKLED ROSE
Rosa rugosa Thunb.
Rose Family

This rose is a large, coarse shrub which usually grows in dense clumps in sea coast thickets, on sand dunes, on islands and along roadsides near the coast. The canes may be as tall as 8 feet and are very prickly as well as hairy.

The shining leaves are dark green and have from 5-9 thick leaflets. These leaflets are furrowed above and prominently ribbed below. The leaf stalks and stipules are hairy. The large flowers may be 3-4 inches broad and have five overlapping petals. The stamens are in a flattened circle around the flattened pistil in the center. The flowers are on short, bristly stalks. The fruit is large and orange, and is very good to eat or to use in jellies. It is rich in vitamin C. The pointed sepals remain on the fruit even when it is ripe.

CINNAMON ROSE
Rosa cinnamomea L.
Rose Family

Cinnamon Rose is sometimes found growing wild where it has spread from cultivation to fields and roadsides. It forms dense thickets up to 6 feet in height and spreads by underground shoots. It is so named, because its fragrance is supposed to suggest cinnamon. The slender, flexible branches are red. They are armed with broad-based, straight or slightly curved *pale-colored prickles* below the stipules. The stipules are broad and have hairy teeth at the margins. The dull-green leaflets are rather small — usually less than one inch (2-4 cm.) long — but occasionally larger on plants which are out in the open. The leaves are paler in color and are downy on the underside. The small *flowers are mostly double* and are pinkish-purple or reddish in color. Blossoms are usually less than 2 inches broad (4-6 cm.) with long, glandless and hairless sepals. Fruit is rarely formed in the wild.

NORTHERN ROSE
Rosa johanensis Fern.
Rose Family

Northern Rose is found in northern Maine on wet, gravelly or rocky banks and on gravelly shores of the St. John River. It is a shrub up to 3 feet (.3-1 m.) in height. The branches are shiny, hairless, and nearly purplish in color. Twigs may have a few bristles but are usually unarmed. There are few or *no prickles* on this rose. The leaves are dark green and somewhat shiny with from 5-9 oval or oval-pointed leaflets. They may have hairs on the nerves on the underside of the leaflets, but are usually hairless. The flowers are either solitary, or in clusters of several. Each is 1½-2½ inches (4-6 cm.) broad and rosy pink in color. The sepals are 1-2 inches (1.5-4 cm.) long and have glandular hairs on them. These sepals remain on the tip of the fruit when it matures. The ripe fruit is smooth, orange-red, nearly round and about ½ inch (1-1.5 cm.) in diameter.

SMOOTH or MEADOW ROSE
Rosa blanda Ait.
Rose Family

This rose grows in dry to moist rocky slopes and shores, and it is usually less than 6 feet high. The canes may have a few prickles, but *are usually smooth*. The leaves are divided into 5-7 toothed, oval leaflets on short stalks. The leaflets are rounded at the tips. The upper surface is a pale, dull green and is not hairy. The stipules at the base of the leaf are rather broad.

The rosy-pink flowers may appear singly or be in a small cluster. The flower stalk and receptacle may be covered with a whitish bloom, but *they are not hairy*. The round fruit is capped by *erect, hairy sepals*.

BEACH PLUM
Prunus maritima Marsh.
Rose Family

Beach Plum is a low, straggling, much-branched shrub usually less than eight feet in height. It grows in sandy soil near the coast, but may be occasionally found in sandy places inland. The young branches are hairy, but become smooth with age. The winter buds are pointed and the bark is dark and close.

The oval or egg-shaped leaves are clustered on projections of the branchlets. The leaves are unlobed, but have margins which are finely-toothed clear to the leaf stalk. The blades have soft hairs on the underside. The white (occasionally pinkish) flowers are ½ to ¾ inch (1.2-2 cm.) broad with five spreading petals and numerous stamens in a tuft in the center. The flowers are in small clusters along the stems, but not in terminal clusters. The flowers expand in April and May before the leaves. The edible fruit is purple or blue-purple, and is used in making jam. The fruit is ½-1 inch (1.3-2.5 cm.) in diameter and is covered with a bloom. The stone inside is usually pointed on both ends with one margin pointed and the other slightly grooved.

WILD or AMERICAN PLUM
Prunus americana Marsh.
Rose Family

Wild Plum is a shrub or small tree up to 30 feet in height. The trunk divides near the ground and it supports many wide-spreading or drooping branches. It grows mostly on bottom-lands and in rich, moist soil at the margins of woods and streams. It is most common from Connecticut southward.

The alternate elliptical or oval leaves sometimes have the widest part above the middle. The base is rounded, the tip is pointed and the margins are sharply or doubly toothed. The firm leaves are rough and dark green on the top, and are hairy and paler in color on the underside. The flowers are ill smelling. They are about 1 inch (1.8-3 cm.) broad and have five white petals with a cluster of stamens inside. The cup-shaped *calyx is red.* The flowers are on slender stalks and are in 2-5 flowered umbels. The fruit is about an inch (2-3 cm.) in diameter. The skin (when ripe) is red, rather thick and tough. The fruit has a tart, yellow flesh and a flattened oval stone. It ripens in August and September.

The bark is light brown-gray with thin scales. The branches are angular or curved. The young twigs are rather stout, greenish and hairy, but later become reddish-brown; they are smooth except for a few round marks (lenticels). The twigs often bear numerous spur-like spines. The *twigs have a bitter taste.*

The brown buds are about 1/3 inch long, broadly conical, and covered with numerous triangular scales which are pale and hairy at the margin. There is no terminal bud.

CANADA PLUM
Prunus nigra Ait.
Rose Family

Canada Plum is a shrub or small tree usually from 6-12 feet, but occasionally up to 30 feet. It has a rather distorted shape. Canada Plum is found chiefly in roadside thickets and at borders of woods. It was formerly planted, and the trees in northern New England may have escaped from these plantings, but it grows wild farther south.

The leaves are very broad and come to an abrupt point. The petioles (leaf stalks) are very stout and the base of the leaves may be rounded or wedge-shaped. The leaves have coarse, spreading, blunt-tipped teeth which are tipped with tiny brown glands that may be seen through a hand lens.

The white flowers are in umbels which open before the leaves do. Each flower has five rounded, white petals which turn pink with age.

The fruit is a thick-skinned edible plum which is sour but is used in cooking. It is light red, orange-red, or yellowish, slightly elongated, and has almost no bloom. Inside is an oval, sharply-ridged stone.

The thin bark is dark brown or gray with slight horizontal markings. The bark becomes scaly and roughened with age. The smooth brown twigs are slender and are at nearly *right angles* to the branchlets. The stems are zigzag and the thorns are about an inch long.

The wood is hard, heavy and close-grained, but is not used commercially.

149

SAND CHERRY
Prunus susquehanae Willd.
Rose Family

    This sand cherry is an *upright shrub* 1-4 feet high. It grows in *acid* sandy or dry, rocky soil, but is not common in northern New England. The firm leaves are not toothed all the way to the base, and the leaf blade narrows as it reaches the leaf stalk. The leaves are at least half as broad as they are long — up to two inches long — and are usually pale beneath. The white flowers appear in May. The small fruit is about one-fourth inch long and is purple-black when ripe. The fruit tapers at the tip and has a large stone inside which is *rounded at the base.*

DWARF SAND CHERRY
Prundus depressa Pursh
(not shown)
Rose Family

    This dwarf sand cherry is a *trailing shrub* which may form low mats 5-6 feet broad. It grows on gravelly or sandy beaches along streams or in limy soils on ledges. The leaves are pale green above and whitened beneath. They have appressed teeth on the margins and the blades are not as firm as those of the above species. The fruit is red-purple to purple-black, and though it tastes sour, it is good to eat. The *stone inside is pointed at both ends.* The new reddish shoots are shiny and take root readily.

PIN, RED, or BIRD CHERRY
Prunus pensylvanica L.
Rose Family

Pin Cherry is a small tree up to 30 feet tall — but usually shorter. It has a very short life span. It turns color in autumn earlier than the choke cherry, and the leaves seem to hang downward. This tree is common in burned or cut-over areas or on ledges and in sparse, rocky woods.

The alternate leaves are very lustrous, narrow, and taper to a point. Fine, even teeth on the margins are tipped with knobbed hairs (glands). The leaves have a bitter taste but an aromatic odor.

The flowers are white, about ½ inch broad and have five round spreading petals. Each flower is on its *own individual stalk*, but these are in *clusters of four or five*, all arising from the same point on the stem.

The fruit is a small, sour, red cherry with a large stone. It is globular, about the size of a pea, and ripens in July. It is good for jelly — if the birds don't eat it first!

The bark is thin, reddish-brown, and is easily removed. The twigs are very slender and shiny. Small buds are clustered at the ends of the twigs.

The wood is soft and is not used commercially.

WILD BLACK or RUM CHERRY

Prunus serotina Ehrh.
Rose Family

Wild Black Cherry is usually 50-75 feet tall, but occasionally reaches heights up to 100 feet. In forest specimens, the trunk is usually long and clean, while specimens growing in the open usually have a short trunk. It is most often found growing with other species in rich soil on fertile slopes. It has a long tap root and requires deep soil.

The alternate, simple, oval-pointed leave are 2-5 inches (3.5-15 cm.) long. They have tapering or rounded base; have margins with rounded teeth; and are rather thick, dark green and shiny on the top surface, but pale underneath. There are usually brown hair along the base of the midrib on the undersid of the leaf.

The white flowers are about ¼ inch (7-1 mm.) across, have five petals, and are arrange in long, cylindrical, drooping clusters 3- inches long. The fruit is a purplish-blacl (when ripe) juicy drupe in rather oper drooping clusters. The seed inside is stony The round drupe, 7-10 mm. in diameter, ma be sweetish or bitter. The calyx has fiv pointed lobes and *remains on the fruit*, whicl is not true of the calyx on the Choke Cherr

Bark on young trunks is smooth, reddish brown and is marked with conspicuou lenticels. The bark peels off in thin film-lik layers to expose the green inner bark whicl has a *distinctive bitter taste but a rathe pleasant odor.* On older trunks the bark i blackish and is roughened by thick, irregula plates with projecting edges. The slende twigs are reddish-brown and the pith is whit or light brown. Buds are smooth and sharp pointed; they are reddish brown with bue scales which are sometimes coated with smoky or grayish film-like skin.

The wood is moderately heavy, hard, an strong. It is fine-grained and does not warp and split when it is seasoned. It is used fo furniture, interior finish, tool handles, an panels.

CHOKE CHERRY
Prunus virginiana L.
Rose Family

Choke Cherry is a common tall shrub or small tree which is usually 10-20 feet high, but occasionally reaches heights up to 30 feet. Frequently two or three trunks will grow together in a clump. This tree will grow in almost any soil and is common along roadsides, near river banks, in abandoned fields, and in rich woods.

The simple, alternate leaves are very thin and are usually *widest above the middle*. They are bright green above and paler below. The blade comes to an abrupt point and has sharp-toothed margins.

The flowers are in thick, white, cylindrical clusters (3-6 inches long) which appear in late spring after the leaves have unfolded. Each flower has five round, spreading petals.

The fruit is a dark red to nearly black drupe with a hard "stone" in the center. Many of these fruits are together in a drooping cluster, but each is on a separate stalk branching from the main central stalk. These fruits ripen in September and become nearly translucent. The *calyx does not remain on the fruit* as it does on that of the Wild Black Cherry. These berries are "puckery" to the taste, but make good jelly.

The bark is dark or smoky gray, rather smooth, but marked with very small, horizontal or rounded wart-like dots of a lighter color. Bark on newer growth peels off easily, but bark on older trees becomes rough and scales off in segments. Twigs are rather stout and are brownish-gray with lighter-colored dots. The twigs have a rank odor when crushed. Buds are 1/6 of an inch long, are sharp-pointed and are covered with from 6-8 visible scales which are purple with tan-colored margins. The wood is heavy, but is not used commercially.

HONEY LOCUST or THORN TREE
Gleditsia triacanthos L.
Legume Family

Honey Locust is a medium-sized tree which is most often seen in cultivation in our area. It is usually 40-50 feet high, but occasionally reaches heights more than 100 feet. The short trunk usually divides into several stout, ascending limbs about 12 feet from the ground. These limbs have many branched thorns on them. The foliage is graceful and lacy-looking. It is common in rich soil of bottom lands outside our area.

The alternate leaves are a dull bluish color. They are compound (and sometimes doubly compound) with from 18 to 28 small, long-oval leaflets.

Inconspicuous flowers are in greenish, pendulous clusters. Male and female flowers are sometimes in separate clusters — often even on different trees.

The fruit is a shiny, leathery, maroon-brown pod 8-16 inches (2-4.5 dm.) long which often *curls spirally* in drying. Inside there are many small, brown, bony seeds. The pods do not split open.

Bark is smooth and dark grayish-brown — on young trees — and is covered with raised, oblong dots (lenticels). On older trees, the bark is rough with broad, jagged, dark-sepia ridges. Bark on the trunk may be covered with thorns. The twigs are rather stout and zigzag, and also bear branched thorns.

The wood is hard, strong, coarse, and durable when in contact with the soil. It is used for fence posts and construction elsewhere, but in New England it is chiefly planted as an ornamental. Some thornless trees have been developed.

SCOTCH BROOM

Cytisus scoparius (L). Link
Legume Family

Scotch Broom is a smooth, stiff-branched shrub from 3-5 feet tall which was introduced and has escaped. It now grows along sandy roadsides or in open woods and barrens. Its angled branches are straight and nearly erect. The well-developed leaves have three small leaflets, but the upper leaves may be reduced to only one leaflet. Sometimes only a few leaves develop and the stems remain bare all summer. The yellow pea-like flowers have two short, broad lips. The flowers are usually solitary on slender stalks in the axils of the older leaves, but they may be paired. The fruit is a long, flat legume (or pea) about two inches long — usually with hairs along the margins. The twigs and small stems are greenish.

BLACK LOCUST or FALSE ACACIA
Robinia pseudo-acacia L.
Legume Family

Black Locust is a medium-sized tree which i usually 30 to 45 feet high in our area. It i native in moist, fertile soil in southern Unitee States, but not in New England. Here it ha been widely introduced and it has escaped ane become established in fields, edges of woods and along roads — usually near habitation.

The alternate, compound leaves are from 8 14 inches long on slender, grooved leaf stalk (peticles) which have swollen bases. There may be from 7 to 21 oblong, stalked leaflet which are rounded at both ends and have untoothed margins.

The showy flowers are creamy-white, very fragrant, and resemble the blossom of a pea The flowers are about an inch wide and are arranged in long, loose, drooping cluster which are 4 or 5 inches (10-13 cm.) long.

The fruit is a small, dark, thin pod from 2-4 inches (5-10 cm.) long and about ½ inch wide The pods contain small, hard, dark brown mottled seeds. The pods often remain on the tree all winter.

Bark on both young and mature trunks is reddish-brown and deeply furrowed with high, rounded ridges which do not peel off in scales. The twigs are rather stout — somewhat zigzag — and often have two spines at the nodes. The buds are imbedded in the twig under the leaf scar between the two stipular spines. The leaf scar often shows three irregular cracks. There are no end buds.

The wood is heavy, very hard and strong, and is very durable when in contact with the soil. It makes good fence posts and is an excellent firewood.

leaf has been greatly reduced

leaf scar
between spines

156

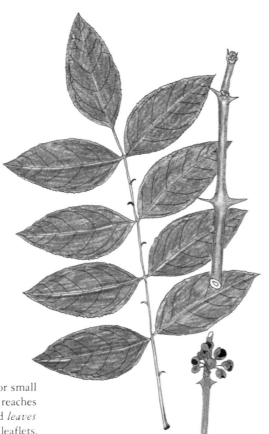

PRICKLY-ASH or
TOOTHACHE-TREE
Xanthoxylum americanum Mill.
Rue Family

Prickly-Ash is a rather rare shrub or small tree which grows in rich woods and reaches heights up to 25 feet. The compound *leaves are alternate* with from 5-11 toothed leaflets. Each leaflet is 1½-2 inches long. Some leaves have small spines. Immature leaflets are downy. This tree is easily confused with Ash, but Ash has opposite leaves instead of alternate. Prickly-Ash also has a characteristic acid odor like lemon. Small greenish-yellow flowers in round clusters about 1 inch in diameter appear in May before the leaves. The fruit is a thick, fleshy, 2-valved pod on a short stalk. The pods split open at maturity to expose the round, shiny black seeds. The branches are smooth, grayish, and have a pair of stipular spines at each node. The bark is used medicinally.

enlarged winter bud
and leaf scar

HOPTREE; WAFER ASH; STINKING ASH

Ptelea trifoliata L.
Rue Family

Hoptree is a shrub or small tree usually less than 20 feet in height. It has eye-catching "wafers" in clusters of 50 or more which cling to the tree after the leaves have fallen. Hoptree grows on rocky slopes or in gravel or alluvial thickets.

The compound leaves are 4-6 inches long and have three leaflets; the end leaflet is the largest. The leaves are on long stalks and the leaflets may have a few rounded teeth on the margins. Young leaves are downy, but become smooth as they mature and have a disagreeable odor — like hops — when they are crushed. Leaves *resemble those on Poison Ivy.*

The flowers are in a spray which appears in early summer. The flowers are small and have five narrow, greenish-white petals. The fruit is a round, flat, winged samara ¾ to 1 inch (2-3 cm.) in diameter. It differs from elm fruits in that there are *two seeds in each fruit.* Fruits are pale yellow-green at first but turn brown with age. Fruits are very bitter and are sometimes used as a substitute for hops.

The bark is dark brown and may be warty or fairly smooth. Twigs are slender and give off a rank odor when broken. Winter buds are blunt, hairy, and are almost surrounded or covered by the raised leaf scar (see insert on drawing). There are no true terminal buds.

The wood is light brown, coarse-grained, rather heavy, and has no commercial value.

BLACK CROWBERRY
Empertrum nigrum L.
Crowberry Family

Crowberry is a low, prostrate, matted shrub which forms a thick, spreading mat over rocks and bare ground. It is an arctic plant which grows at higher elevations or on ocean cliffs and banks, and rarely reaches heights over six inches. Numerous needle-like leaves are crowded in the stems. The leaves are less than ¼ inch long, and tiny inconspicuous flowers are lost among these leaves. The minute flowers have three sepals and three petals, are pink only near the base, and are predominantly creamy-green. The fruit is a black, berry-like drupe which ripens in July. The berry is edible, but it is rather dry and tasteless.

PURPLE CROWBERRY
Empetrum atropurpureum Fern. & Wieg.
Crowberry Family

Purple Crowberry is a low, trailing shrub similar to the one above. The tiny, linear leaves are cob-webby with white hairs and stand erect when they first expand. When mature, the leaves spread wide. The fruits are red or purple-black and are dull instead of shiny. This crowberry usually grows near granite on the northern mountains but may be found in acid gravel near the coast. It blooms in early summer.

1. male flowers
2. female flowers are almost concealed by upper leaves

BROOM CROWBERRY
Corema conradii Torr.
Crowberry Family

Broom Crowberry is also called Poverty Grass by some. It is a much-branched shrub 5-22 inches high. (1.5-6 dm.) It is not a common shrub, but it does grow in sterile soil mostly near the coast. Look for it in sandy pine-barrens, sandhills, and especially in sand containing silica.

The tiny leaves are narrow and about ¼ inch (4-6 mm.) long. They are crowded on the stems. When mature, they are smooth and bright deep green in color. The flowers are in tiny clusters at the tips of the upright branches. Female and male flowers are usually on separate plants. Each tiny flower is in the axil of a scaly bract. There will be three stamens or three pistils depending upon the sex of the flower. The male plants are quite handsome when in flower because of the tufted purple filaments and the brown-purple anthers. The fruit is a very tiny, dry, drupe with three (occasionally 4-5) nutlets inside.

STAGHORN SUMAC
Rhus typhina L.
Sumac Family

Staghorn Sumac is a shrub or small, irregular tree usually reaching heights of only 10-20 feet, but occasionally reaching heights up to 45 feet. The trunk is short and has a broad, flat-topped crown. Staghorn Sumac

160

tends to grow in large clumps and is common throughout New England, especially in old pastures and open areas. It never grows in deep woods. Sumacs with red fruit *are not poisonous* — in fact, red lemonade can be made from Staghorn Sumac.

The alternate, compound leaves may be from 16-24 inches (4-6 dm.) long and have from 11-31 leaflets. These leaflets are from 2-5 inches (5-13 cm.) long, have pointed tips and toothed margins, and are rounded or heart-shaped at the base.

The flowers appear in May or June and occur in dense, yellow-green pointed clusters. Male and female flowers are in separate clusters — sometimes on separate trees. The female clusters are from 5-8 inches (1.2-2 dm.) long and the male clusters are from 8-12 inches (2-3 dm.) long. Only trees with female flowers produce fruit.

The fruit is arranged on compact, erect, cone-like, maroon clusters which are from 5-8 inches (1.2-2 dm.) long. A single fruit is a round drupe covered with red hairs and containing a small, hard seed.

Bark on old trunks is dark brown and is sometimes scaly. Bark on younger trunks and branches is smooth, thin, rather papery, and is covered with numerous lenticels or rough dots. The twigs are covered with brown or black velvet. If the twigs are cut, a milky juice will come out. The buds are alternate, conical, and covered with dense, rusty hairs. There is no terminal bud.

The wood is brittle, soft, orange-colored and beautifully grained and satiny to the touch. It is sometimes used for cabinet work, but most often used in the manufacture of fancy boxes and souvenirs, darning eggs and the like.

greatly reduced

SMOOTH SUMAC
Rhus glabra L.
Sumac Family

   Smooth Sumac is similar to, but smaller than, Staghorn Sumac. It is a shrubby tree from 2-10 feet in height. It grows in dry soil in fields and openings in woods. The leaves are divided into many toothed, pointed leaflets attached to a central rib. Each leaflet is 2-4 inches long. The underside is quite whitish, and the *leaf stalks are hairless.* The flowers are in a pyramidal cluster which opens in July and August. The fruits are red and are covered with short hairs. The fruit stalks are usually hairless and are covered with a slight bloom. The smooth twigs are somewhat flattened.

no hairs

greatly reduced leaf

DWARF or SHINING SUMAC
Rhus copallina L.
Sumac Family

   This sumac grows in rocky hills from southern Maine southward. It is only a shrub at the northern part of its range, but becomes a small tree up to 30 feet in height farther south. The branches, leaf stalks, and flower stalks have minute ash-colored hairs. The sap is watery instead of milky white like the sap of Staghorn Sumac. The twigs also taste something like turpentine. The leaves have 9-21 (usually 17) smooth, shining, nearly always toothless leaflets. The compound leaf may be 6-12 inches long. *Note the wings* along the main leaf rib between the leaflets. Poison Sumac does not have these. The flowers are in a dense panicle similar to those of Staghorn Sumac.

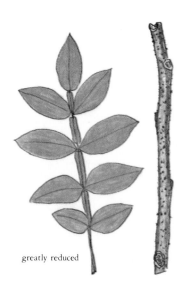

greatly reduced

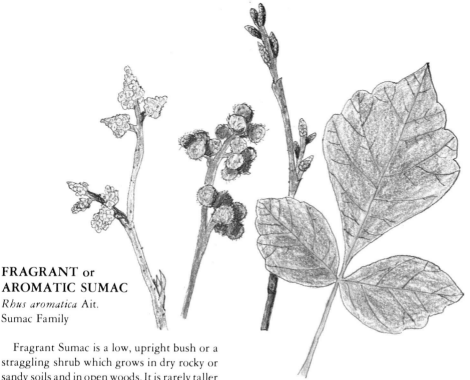

FRAGRANT or AROMATIC SUMAC
Rhus aromatica Ait.
Sumac Family

Fragrant Sumac is a low, upright bush or a straggling shrub which grows in dry rocky or sandy soils and in open woods. It is rarely taller than 7 feet. The shrub is highly variable, but it is *the only sumac with winter catkins.* Twigs and leaves are pungently aromatic when crushed.

The leaves may be from 4-6 inches long and have three leaflets. The end leaflet is larger than the two side ones, is on a short stalk, and is *toothed above the middle only.*

The small greenish or pale yellow flowers are clustered in dense upright clusters at the twig tips. The catkins form in late summer and expand in spring before the leaves do. The round fruits are closely covered with long, soft, red hairs and are arranged in small clusters. The stone inside is compressed but has convex sides.

The twigs are brown and the bark is smooth. The leaf buds are hidden under the round leaf scars.

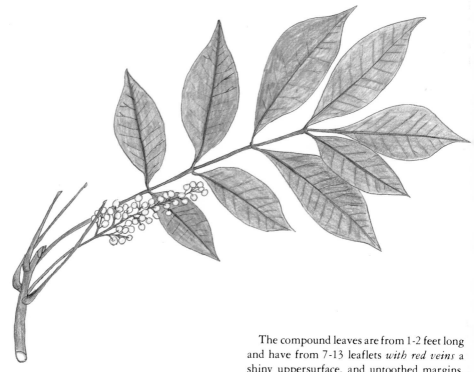

POISON SUMAC
Rhus vernix L.
Sumac Family

Poison Sumac is quite scarce in our area, and is almost exclusively found in swamps and wet areas where the average person is not likely to be. It is a shrub or small tree usually less than ten feet in height with a round-topped — not flat — head. The skin irritant is *worse than Poison Ivy* and it is especially poisonous at the time of bloom.

The compound leaves are from 1-2 feet long and have from 7-13 leaflets *with red veins* a shiny uppersurface, and untoothed margins. The base of the leaflets is wedge-shaped and the bottom surface is paler in color.

The small, yellow-green flowers are in open, drooping clusters. Male and female flowers are on different plants, so fruit will not be produced on a tree unless it contains female flowers.

The fruits are off-white, glossy berry-like drupes in open sprays. They ripen in September, and may remain on the tree into the winter.

The thin bark is smooth, somewhat streaked and has rough, horizontally-elongated marks called lenticels. The twigs are stout, orange-brown at first but later turning to light gray. They are often glossy and are

164

covered with numerous raised lenticels. The pith on the inside is yellow-brown. If broken, the twigs will emit a watery juice which will turn yellow upon exposure. Purplish, pointed buds are alternate and the terminal buds are larger than the others.

The wood is not used commercially.

POISON IVY or
POISON MERCURY
Rhus radicans L.
Sumac Family

Poison Ivy may be a low, trailing plant or a high climbing vine with aerial, clinging roots. It is often a roadside weed and occurs in open woods, thickets, and along paths and fences.

The compound leaf has three leaflets with very pointed tips. The terminal leaflet is on a longer stalk than the other two. The margins may be toothless or have large, uneven teeth. The flowers are yellowish-green in clusters in axils of past year's leaves. The fruit is a dry, whitish drupe. The outside peels off readily to expose the inside. The leaves, flowers, fruit, and smoke from burning plants are very poisonous to the skin of many people and cause a painful rash.

BLACK ALDER or WINTERBERRY
Ilex verticillata (L.) Gray
Holly Family

Black Alder is a shrub which grows to heights of from 3-10 feet. There are several forms of *Ilex verticillata* with small differences in the leaves which make exact identification difficult for a beginner. This shrub is common in New England in swamps, bogs, thickets, and on shores of streams and ponds.

The alternate leaves are variable, up to three inches long with distinct, coarse teeth on the margins. Though leaf shape varies, it is usually broadest at or above the middle. Leaves are usually dull on the upper side — but some bushes may have shiny leaves. Leaves on some bushes may have hairs on the underside while the leaves on other bushes may not. If a hand lens is used, tiny, transparent dots may be seen on the leaves of some varieties of this shrub.

Inconspicuous white flowers are borne in clusters or singly and are *attached directly to the stem*. The flowers open in June, and often male and female flowers will occur on separate shrubs.

A brilliant orange-scarlet berry about ¼ inch in diameter — either solitary or in clusters — is seated directly on the stem. These berries remain on the twigs after the leaves fall and make good Christmas decorations especially when added to outdoor Christmas wreaths.

The bark is smooth, dull gray on the stems and branches and a warm pale gray on the twigs.

SMOOTH WINTERBERRY
Ilex laevigata (Pursh) Gray
Holly Family

Smooth Winterberry is similar to *I. verticillata* and is not easily distinguished from it. It is an upright shrub 3-10 feet in height which grows in swampy woods or peaty areas. It is not as common as *I. verticillata* and does not grow north of southern Maine.

The branches are smooth. The shining, alternate, simple leaves are pointed at both the tip and the base, and the margins have teeth which point towards the tip. The underside of the leaf is usually smooth, but may be hairy on the veins only. Leaves turn yellow in the fall before falling. Small flowers may have either four or five petals and are on short stalks. Some of the male flowers have slender stalks more than ½ inch long, while those on *I. verticillata* are very short. The orange-red fruits are larger (nearly ½ inch in diameter) and are on stalks — not seated directly on the stem as are the fruits on *I. verticillata*. The calyx remains on the fruit and the fruit will remain on the branchlets after it is mature.

INKBERRY

Ilex glabra (L.) Gray
Holly Family

Inkberry is a shrub 2-6 feet in height which grows in peaty soil or in low sandy soil along the coast. It is rare in northern New England, but it does occur on Isle au Haut in Maine and in one locality in southern New Hampshire. The alternate, narrow leaves have blunt tips, dots on the underside, and may have a few obscure teeth near the tip of the blade. Leaves are 1-2 inches long. The leaves are shiny, evergreen, and rather leathery in texture. The small white flowers open in early summer. Male flowers are on long stalks — several together in a cluster. Female flowers are solitary on stalks arising from the leaf axils. The fruits are berry-like drupes containing 4-9 small nutlets. The fruits are usually solitary in axils of leaves. They become black when mature, are firm, dry, and remain on the twig. Leaf stalks and twigs both have minute, ashy-gray hairs on them.

MOUNTAIN HOLLY

Nemopanthus mucronata (L.) Trel.
Holly Family

Mountain Holly is a slender, erect shrub from 6-15 feet tall. It grows in damp thickets, bogs, or swamps. It is frequent throughout all mountain regions and wooded hills of northern New England, but is rarer near the coast and farther south. It grows to elevations up to 3000 feet, but does not grow in alpine areas.

There are many small leaves on this shrub. They are thin, elliptic with *a single sharp point at the tip,* and have a base which tapers toward the leaf stalk. Leaves are smooth, have a slender, purplish stalk, toothless margins, and are light green in color.

The small flowers are white or yellowish, and each is on a separate, slender flower stalk about an inch long. These may be solitary or in small clusters at the base of the leaves and bloom in May. Each flower has 4 or 5 narrow petals.

The fruit is a red, berry-like drupe containing several seeds. It has a distinct color — light crimson red, but not scarlet and is not shiny. The fruit ripens in August and early September.

Bark on older branches is ashen gray, smooth, and is sparingly marked with elongated brown dots. The buds are sharp-pointed and are a purplish color.

BURNING BUSH

Euonymus atropurpurea Jacq.
Stafftree Family

Burning Bush is a large shrub or a small tree which reaches heights up to 25 feet. It grows in rich woods and thickets elsewhere, but when found in New England, it has usually escaped from cultivation. The purple flowers are 1/4-1/3 inch wide with four petals. The short stamens are borne on the edge of the flat, broad disk in the center. The four (or 5) sepals are united at the base and form a short, flat calyx. Usually from 7-15 flowers are in each long-stalked cluster.

The leaves are opposite, oblong or pointed, and the margins of the larger leaves may have fine teeth. Leaves have stalks and are usually hairy on the underside, and vary in length from 1½ to 5 inches.

The fruit is a distinctive purple-red, smooth, four-lobed capsule. The seeds inside are brown, but have a scarlet covering.

EUROPEAN SPINDLE TREE
Euonymus europaeus L.
Stafftree Family

This *Euonymus* is similar to Burning Bush, but the leaves are usually smaller and they are *not hairy*. The margins have fine teeth. The flowers are yellow-green, have four (rarely 5) petals, and are in clusters of only 2-5. The four-lobed fruit capsule is pink, but the seeds inside have orange coverings.

Spindle Tree is not common in northern New England, but it has occasionally escaped from cultivation to roadsides and waste places near habitation.

CLIMBING BITTERSWEET or WAXWEED
Celastrus scandens L.
Stafftree Family

This is a vine-like shrub up to thirty feet high with a woody, twining stem up to one inch thick. It may climb on near-by trees and shrubs or trail along the ground if there is no support. It grows in thickets, along overgrown walls and fences, near the coast and along river banks.

The alternate, oblong leaves have finely-toothed margins and pointed tips. They have short leaf stalks and are 2-4 inches long.

Small, greenish or cream-colored flowers appear in June. They are small and inconspicuous, but are arranged in raceme-like clusters.

The pod is orange colored and is globular with a point at the outer end. This outer skin *curls backward in three divisions* to display the beautiful scarlet covering on the seeds inside.

The stems are smooth and buff gray. The wood is not commercially used, but the shrub is often cultivated and sold commercially for the ornamental fruits which are used in flower arrangements.

BLADDERNUT
Staphylea trifolia L.
Bladdernut Family

Bladdernut is an upright shrub or small tree usually not more than 15 feet in height. It grows in rich thickets, along borders of woods and in fertile soil along roadsides from Massachusetts southward.

The whitish, bell-shaped flowers are on hairy stalks with bracts at the base. The flower stalks are united to form drooping clusters. Usually there are five petals which do not spread wide, but the number varies — always agreeing with the number of green sepals which overlap the flower.

Young leaves may be hairy — but mature leaves are not. Leaves are compound with 3 pointed, toothed leaflets — each 1½-2½ inches in length.

The fruits are inflated, papery capsules 1-2 inches (2-5 cm.) long. This pod splits open when ripe into three pointed lobes. Occasionally a pod may have four lobes.

The bark of older branches is greenish or gray-streaked-with-white. Light, warm-gray *stems are conspicuously green striped.* The twigs are green, slender, and may have a few small wart-like lenticels. The pith is white and narrow. The buds are brown, small, and have 2-4 scales.

1. terminal bud
2. a twig showing leaf scar and stalked bud
3. winged fruit

1.　　2.

MOUNTAIN MAPLE

Acer spicatum Lam.
Maple Family

Mountain Maple is a small, bushy tree seldom over 30 feet in height which sometimes forms rather dense thickets because it tends to grow in clumps. This tree grows best on damp, northern slopes or in cool, mountain woods.

Thin, opposite leaves are three-lobed and rather hairy on the lower surface — especially at the ribs. There are rounded teeth on the margins and the veins on the top surface of the leaves have a sunken appearance. The leaves turn brilliant red in late summer and autumn.

The flowers appear in June in long, hairy greenish-yellow clusters after the leaves are nearly full grown. The paired, winged fruit occurs in clusters. There is a wrinkled depression on the seed body and the wings spread slightly. This fruit is ¾ of an inch or less (1.5-2.5 cm.) in length and turns red in mid-summer.

The bark is reddish brown to gray in color. It is thin and somewhat furrowed or flaky. The twigs are slender, hairy, and reddish on the upper surface, but *are not striped*. The pith is brown. The buds are hairy, slender, pointed, and slightly stalked.

The wood is soft, light, and close-grained, but it is seldom used commercially.

172

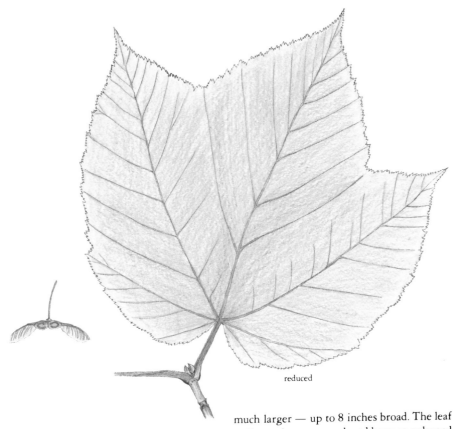

reduced

STRIPED MAPLE or MOOSE WOOD

Acer pensylvanicum L.
Maple Family

Striped Maple is a small tree usually 10-25 feet tall, but it reaches heights up to 40 feet. The trunk is usually short and divides into slender, straight branches which form a deep and broad crown. This tree prefers moist, cool, shaded, often rocky mountain slopes.

The large, opposite, simple leaves have three lobes, finely toothed margins, and a heart-shaped base. They are usually about six inches long, but leaves on new growth may be much larger — up to 8 inches broad. The leaf stalks are long, grooved, and have an enlarged base.

Flowers appear in May or June after the leaves are full grown. Male and female flowers occur on the same tree, but in different clusters. The paired, winged fruits are also in drooping clusters. The wings are very thin, spread wide, and may be nearly an inch long.

The bark on newer trees has white and green *longitudinal streaks*. Later the bark becomes rougher and less streaked. The twigs are at first green, but later turn red with a few lenticels. The glossy, angular buds are opposite, large, stalked, and taper to a blunt point. The wood is soft, close-grained and porous and is seldom used commercially.

enlarged winter buds

NORWAY MAPLE

Acer platonoides L.
Maple Family

Norway Maple is a European species which has been widely planted along city streets as a shade tree. It reaches heights up to 100 feet and has a round head. A sure way to identify this maple is by the drop of *milky sap at the base of the leaf stalk* when it is broken from the tree. Also, the maple keys have wings which are at the widest angle of all the common maples.

The large five-lobed leaves may be as wide as seven inches. The blades are very similar to, but have a firmer texture than, the Sugar Maple, and have more sharply-tipped lobes. The flowers are yellowish or light green and appear before the foliage. They are in spreading clusters.

The reddish-brown end buds are very conspicuous. Sometimes they are a deep olive green at the base.

ROCK, HARD or SUGAR MAPLE
Acer saccharum Marsh.
Maple Family

Sugar Maple is a large tree which reaches heights of 100 feet or more. The trunk is without branches for quite a way up, and the crown is short and spreading. It is common throughout northern New England and grows best in well-drained upland soils.

The opposite, simple leaves are usually five-lobed with *rounded sinuses* between the pointed lobes. They may be from 3-6 inches (.8-2 dm.) broad and are often *wider than they are long*. They have a thin texture, are bright green above and a pale green underneath.

The flowers are yellow-green without petals. Both male and female flowers are in long drooping clusters — but not in the same cluster. The flowers appear in May when the leaves develop.

The fruit does not mature until September which is later than the fruit of the Red and Silver Maples which mature in early summer. The fruit is paired and winged — 1-1½ inches (2.5-4 cm.) long. The seed body is nearly spherical.

Bark on young trees is smooth and pale; on older trees it is gray and deeply furrowed into long, irregular plates or flakes which often loosen vertically along the side. The twigs are slender, smooth, and reddish-brown, and are covered with numerous pale markings.

Sugar Maple is a valuable tree. The hard wood with close grain is used for flooring, furniture, and interior finish. The sap is high in sugar content and is collected for maple syrup and sugar. Wood from this tree makes an excellent firewood.

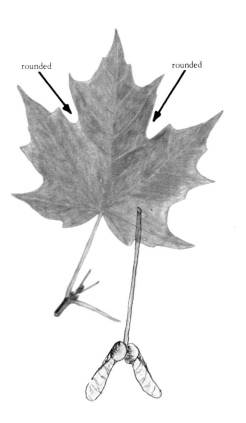

rounded   rounded

RED or SWAMP MAPLE
Acer rubrum L.
Maple Family

Red Maple is a medium-sized tree 50-75 feet tall with upright branches which form a rather narrow head. Usually the trunk is not divided. It is a rapid-growing tree which is planted as an ornamental. It is typically found in swamps and poorly-drained places, but is often found in a variety of drier habitats.

The opposite leaves have from 3-5 lobes and the sinus between the pointed lobes has *a sharp angle* — not rounded as on the Sugar Maple. The upper surface is light green and the lower surface is whitish. There are sharp, irregular teeth on the margins and the blade has a long leaf stalk.

The flowers are in clusters on stalks which appear in April before the leaf buds open. Male flowers are yellow-red and female flowers are bright scarlet. Usually male and female flowers occur on different trees.

The fruit is paired and winged, and germinates soon after it falls. The wings are slightly divergent, are about ¾ inch (2 cm.) long, and are broadest at or above the middle. The seed body does not have a definite depression as do those of the Striped and Mountain Maples.

Bark on young trees is smooth and light gray; on older trunks it is dark gray, ridged, and broken into plate-like scales or ridges. Twigs are straight, stiff, and reddish in color and are odorless when bruised. The buds may be clustered.

The wood is close-grained, heavy, and moderately strong. It is not durable, but will take a good polish. It is mainly used for pulp, pallets, furniture stock, canoe paddles, and fuel. Sugar content in the sap is not as high as in that of Sugar Maple, but it is also used in making maple syrup.

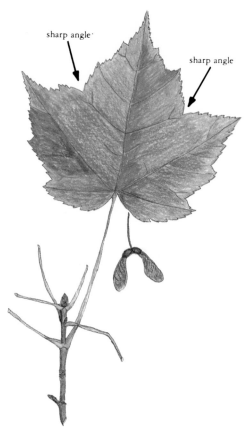

sharp angle

sharp angle

SILVER, RIVER or WHITE MAPLE
Acer saccharinum L.
Maple Family

rounded

Silver Maple is a quite large ornamental tree which is fairly common, except perhaps near the coast. It grows on river banks and bottom lands and reaches heights of 60-80 feet. It prefers moist, deep soil, but will grow in drier locations.

The leaves are very deeply and narrowly five-lobed with rather deep incisions (sinuses) with rounded bases. The leaves are silvery white (downy when young) on the underside. The leaves turn yellow in autumn.

The flowers are greenish-yellow or reddish and appear earlier than those of Scarlet Maple. They are in dense, stemless clusters. The winged fruit is usually hairy at the base. It is pale colored and from 1½-2½ inches (4-6 cm.) long, and matures in the spring. The seed body is rather large and football shaped. One fruit of a pair frequently does not develop.

The bark on young trees is smooth, gray, and slightly tinged with red. On older trees it is red-brown, furrowed, and separated into thin scales. The branches are long, slender and pendulous, and the twigs are often *curved upward at the tip* — orange or reddish above and green below. The twigs are red-orange to shiny chestnut-brown and give off a rank odor when they are crushed. The buds are reddish and round-tipped.

The wood is softer than that of hard maple. It is close-grained, not durable, and is easily worked, but if harvested in New England, it usually is used for pulp. This tree is often planted as an ornamental.

winter bud

BOX ELDER or ASH-LEAF MAPLE

Acer negundo L.
Maple Family

Box Elder is a medium-sized tree which reaches heights up to 50 feet or so. The trunk is usually short and divided into stout (sometimes drooping) branches which form a deep, broad crown. This tree thrives best in moist soil and is commonly found along streams or along borders of lakes and swamps.

The opposite, compound leaves have 3-5 coarsely- and irregularly-toothed leaflets. The leaflets are pointed and veiny, usually deep green or a light olive green.

Flowers appear in April. Male and female flowers occur on different trees. The fruit is double and winged and is arranged in large, drooping clusters which mature in September and remain on the tree in the winter.

Bark on branches and young trunks is smooth and grayish-brown; on older trees it is thick with distinct narrow ridges. Twigs are stout, purplish-green or green and may be smooth or covered with a whitish bloom and scattered, raised marks (lenticels). Buds are hairy, opposite, large, and short-stalked. The terminal bud is more pointed than the others.

The wood is not heavy or durable, and is of little commercial importance. It is sometimes used for pulp and in the making of inexpensive furniture. It is a rapidly-growing tree and is often planted as an ornamental on lawns, along roads, and in parks.

OHIO BUCKEYE
Aesculus glabra Willd.
Buckeye Family

Ohio Buckeye is a small tree which rarely grows as high as 50 feet. It has a short, slender trunk with wide-spreading limbs and branches. It is not common in New England, but it has been planted occasionally and does survive.

The opposite leaves have 5-7 (usually 5) leaflets which all radiate from the same central point. The *foliage is ill-smelling* when bruised. The leaflets have unevenly or doubly-toothed margins, tapered points, are yellow-green and 4-6 inches long.

The flowers are clustered together in downy panicles about five or six inches long. Each flower has four long, light green-yellow petals which do not spread open. The stamens are longer than and protrude from the center of the petals.

The fruit is a thick round or pear-shaped capsule which usually contains only one somewhat flattened, shiny brown, nut-like seed; occasionally the capsule will contain two seeds. The young fruit is covered with spines, but as it matures it becomes warty. Fruit matures in October.

The bark is gray-brown, rough, has slight perpendicular seams, and *a fetid odor.* The twigs are downy and brown at first, then become smooth and reddish-brown to ashy-gray. The pith is large, light green, and round in general outline. The buds are opposite, sharp-pointed, and covered with nearly triangular scales.

The wood is weak, soft, and light colored. It is not commercially valuable in New England.

greatly reduced

179

greatly reduced

HORSECHESTNUT

Aesculus hippocastanum L.
Buckeye Family

Horsechestnut is a beautiful, symmetrical tree which has been planted as an ornamental in New England. Here it grows up to 80 feet, but in its native Europe and Asia, it is much taller. The trunk usually divides into several strong limbs about 10 feet above the ground and these support a broad, spreading crown. This tree makes a good shade tree, but it needs rich soil to grow well.

The opposite, dark green compound leaves are very large. Seven wedge-shaped leaflets *radiate from a central point*. The margins have coarse teeth, and the blades abruptly come to a point. The widest part of the leaflet is *above the middle*. Each leaflet is 4-8 inches long.

Flowers are in erect, showy, terminal clusters. Individual flowers have five white petals which are spotted with yellow or *madder* purple.

The fruit is a round pod 1-1½ inches (2.5-4 cm.) in diameter with rigid, scattered spines or prickles. It is green at first, but ripens to a rusty brown. The pod contains a single, shining nut-like seed which is not edible.

The bark is dull, amber brown with flat, irregularly set scales. The branches and twigs are stout and coarse. Winter buds are large, very gummy, and nearly black in color.

The wood is light, soft, and close-grained. It is not used commercially in New England, but it is used in its native Europe.

ALDER-LEAVED BUCKTHORN

Rhamnus alnifolia L'Her.
Buckthorn Family

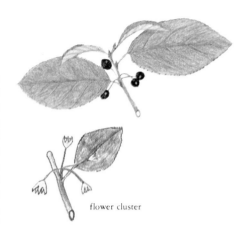

This bush grows in swamps and wet, bushy meadows to heights of from 2-4 feet. It has alternate, narrow leaves with prominent veins and fine scalloped teeth at the margins. The elliptical leaves are 2-4 inches long. Small greenish flowers with no petals appear in late May on long stalks at the base of the leaf stalks.

Fruits are black berries about ¼ inch in diameter. They grow in clusters on long stems and have 3 flat, scarcely-grooved seeds inside.

The gray or gray-brown stems are nearly smooth and quite thornless.

flower cluster

COMMON or EUROPEAN BUCKTHORN

Rhamnus cathartica L.
Buckthorn Family

Common Buckthorn is a small tree or a coarse shrub rarely as tall as twenty feet. It is not native to our area, but has escaped from cultivation and has become naturalized along fences, or at the edges of thickets and woods.

The leaves are usually opposite with a few being alternate. On some plants, the leaves will be in clusters of from 3 to 6. The leaves are broadly elliptic and hairless, and have fine-toothed margins and *prominent curving veins*. Each is 1½-2½ inches long.

The small greenish flowers have four petals and stamens. They are clustered together and appear in May. The fruit is black and berrylike, 1/3 inch in diameter with three or four seeds with a deep, narrow dorsal groove.

The twigs are dark brown and unlined. The bark is sepia brown, rough, and has confluent ridges and yellow inner bark. The twigs often will *end in a single sharp thorn*.

thorn

enlarged
twig tip

SMOOTH or
GLOSSY BUCKTHORN
Rhamnus frangula L.
Buckthorn Family

Smooth Buckthorn is a shrub or small tree which reaches heights of nearly twenty feet. It is a native of Europe, but has been planted in New England and is rapidly becoming naturalized along fence rows and in thickets. Young branches are hairy at the nodes. New twigs are red-brown with long tan dots while older twigs are gray-brown. The alternate leaves are short-oblong to roundish with the broadest part at or above the middle. The blade has a short, abrupt tip. Mature leaves are from 1-3 inches (3-7 cm.) long. They have prominent veins and the margins may be untoothed or have inconspicuous teeth. Winter buds are small and uncovered. Small flowers on smooth stalks appear in clusters in May. Each flower is on a cup-shaped disk and has five notched petals. The fruit is a black, 2-seeded, berry-like drupe. The seeds are not furrowed.

NEW JERSEY TEA or RED-ROOT
Ceanothus americanus L.
Buckthorn Family

New Jersey Tea is a low shrub with several erect and branching stems arising from a deep reddish root. This bush is seldom taller than three feet, and grows in dry, open woods and along roadsides.

The pointed leaves are on long leaf stalks, have toothed margins and rounded bases, and have three main veins running lengthwise. Each leaf is 1-3 inches long.

Numerous tiny white flowers are in elongated, woolly clusters which are about an inch long and have long stalks. The claws of the petals are very narrow.

The fruit is a dry, roundish pod or capsule which splits into three parts when it is ripe. The fruit is nearly black, and is depressed at the tip.

This plant has been used as a substitute for tea.

WESTERN NEW JERSEY TEA
Ceanothus ovatus Desf.
Buckthorn Family

Western New Jersey Tea is a low shrub up to 3 feet (1 m.) high with slender, woody upright branches. It grows on sandy or rocky plains, prairies and slopes. The yellow-green leaves are long-oval with rounded points at both ends. The margins have small rounded or forward-pointing teeth. Teeth on young leaves may be gland-tipped. There are *3 main veins* which originate at the base of the leaf. Leaves vary in size from 1-3½ inches (2.5-6 cm.) in length and may be slightly hairy on the underside. The flower clusters are on short *leafless stalks* at the tips of the leafy branches. The fruit is a dark brown, dry, round capsule. It has a 3-part top in a cup.

enlarged fruit

typical leaf

reduced

no disks at
tips of tendrils

greatly reduced

WOODBINE or
VIRGINIA CREEPER
Parthenocissus quinquefolia L. Planch.
Vine Family

Woodbine is a high-climbing or trailing woody vein which climbs by means of adhesive disks at the ends of the tendrils. The leaf stalks, flower stalks, and twigs are usually red. It grows in woods and on rocky banks.

The compound leaves have five, toothed leaflets arranged around a central point at the end of a long leaf stalk. Each leaflet is 2-6 inches long and is narrowed at the base and coarsely toothed — at least above the middle. The upper surface is dull or dark green and the under surface is paler in color. The mid veins are often red.

Small greenish flowers have five thick, concave petals. These flowers are arranged in an erect and spreading cluster containing anywhere from a few to two hundred flowers. The fruit is a berry which turns blue in October. Each berry has from 1-3 seeds. The twigs are hairless and the pith inside is white. Winter buds are covered with scales. The bark is tight and often dotted.

VIRGINIA CREEPER or
WOODBINE
Parthenocissus inserta K.
Vine Family

This woodbine is similar to *P. quinquefolia*. It is a loosely-climbing, leaning, or trailing vine with tendrils having 3-5 slender-tipped, twining *branches without disks*, while the preceding creeper climbs by means of adhesive disks at the tips of the tendrils. The foliage is a shiny grass-green on top and is divided into five pointed, toothed leaflets which are usually 2-4½ inches long. (On another form of this plant, *Parthenocissus inserta* forma *macrophylla*, the leaflets are up to eight inches long and four inches wide.)

The flowers are usually in long-stalked, branching clusters with 10-60 flowers. The spreading cluster has no central axis. This woodbine usually has a pair of nearly equal, green spreading branches with a brown or tan bud in the crotch. This woodbine grows in woods, thickets, borders of streams and on rocky slopes and is common throughout northern New England — except for northern Maine. The fruit is a rather hard berry about ¼ inch in diameter with 3-4 seeds inside. In winter, this plant is recognized by its climbing tendrils and close bark.

FOX GRAPE
Vitis labrusca L.
Vine Family

greatly reduced

This grape is a high climber which ascends large trees. A mature vine may have a main stem a foot in diameter. It grows in wet or dry thickets and at borders of woods. The young leaves are densely felted with whitish or rusty-red hairs which will remain on the underside when the leaves mature. Mature leaves are thick and strong-veined. The leaves on fruiting vines have forward-pointing lobes with toothed margins. Each leaf will be opposite a forked tendril or a flower cluster.

The tiny flowers are in compact, drooping clusters. The grapes are in clusters of 20 or fewer. They vary in color and may be purple, blackish, red, brown, or yellow. One variety of this grape has white grapes. The grapes become sweet when they are ripe. The forked twigs and branchlets are felted with rusty hairs. The pith inside the twigs is brown. The loose bark on older vines separates into strips.

greatly reduced

SILVERLEAF GRAPE
Vitis aestivalis Michx.
Vine Family

On this grape, the young branchlets and the leafstalks have *rusty or reddish woolly hairs*. There is no tendril or flower cluster opposite every third leaf. Most of the leaves have 3-6 lobes. The grapes are black with a thin whitish bloom. Each grape is ¼-½ inch in diameter and has an acid taste. This high climbing grape grows in dry woods and thickets.

Vitis aestivals var. argentifolia
The branchlets and leafstalks on this grape are smooth, but are *covered with a whitened bloom*. The leaves are stongly whitened on the underside. New leaves may be slightly hairy, but they soon become smooth — except perhaps on the ribs on the underside of the leaf.

RIVER, FROST, WINTER or CHICKEN GRAPE
Vitus riparia Michx.
Vine Family

This grape grows on banks of rivers, in rich thickets, or near water. It is a high-climbing vine with alternate, shining, light green leaves and tendrils between the leaves. Every third leaf usually lacks a tendril or a flower cluster.

The leaves have sharp, triangular to long-tapering teeth and from 3-7 sharp-pointed lobes. The leaves are green underneath, and may have a few hairs or none at all.

186

The tiny, white fragrant flowers are in long, compound clusters on a long stalk arising at the leaf axils. The fruits are in crowded clusters. They are about ½ inch in diameter and are bluish-black with a bluish powder on them. They are quite sweet farther west, but here in the northeast they are likely to be sour until the frost hits, at which time they become sweet. They ripen in September.

greatly reduced

NEW ENGLAND GRAPE

Vitis novae-angliae Fern.
Vine Family

New England Grape is a vigorous climber which grows in rich thickets. Though occasionally found in central Maine, it often does not set fruit in that area. It has not been found in northern and eastern Maine, and is more common in southern New England. The young new twigs are reddish and hairy. Young, expanding leaves are densely felted, but become smooth and hairless as they mature. The mature leaf blades may be nearly square in general outline, while smaller ones may be roundish and taper to a point. Leaves may be unlobed or merely "shouldered" and vary in size from 2½ to 7 inches (.7-1.8 dm.). The tendrils or flower clusters appear on three to five axils in a row, not alternating as on other grapes. The grapes are around ½ inch (1.2-1.7 cm.) in diameter and are purple black with a whitish covering. They have a sharply acid taste.

greatly reduced

BASSWOOD or
BASSWOOD LINDEN

Tilia americana L.
Linden Family

Basswood is a tall tree from 60-100 feet in height. It can be identified by the odd way in which clusters of flowers and fruit hang from the center of very narrow leaf-like bracts. Basswood grows in rich woods, but is often planted as a shade tree on lawns and along city streets.

The simple, alternate leaves are very large and hairless. The blades are unequally heart-shaped at the base and have margins with sharp teeth with slender tips. The leaves may be from 5-8 inches (.7-2 dm.) long and 3-4 inches (.8-1 dm.) wide.

Small clusters of fragrant, creamy-white flowers hang on hairless flower stalks. The flowers are ½ inches (1.-1.5 cm.) across and have five yellowish petals. They appear in July, and bees make a very flavorful honey from their nectar.

The fruit is a stalked cluster of small, round, pale green nutlets which are attached to a leafy wing which may be ½-1 inch (1.3-2.2 cm.) wide and 2-4 inches (5-10 cm.) long. The clusters of dried nutlets remain on the trees after the leaves have fallen.

The bark on older branches and the trunk is ridged and furrowed. The hairless twigs are green to red-gray becoming dark gray. The winter buds are dark red. The wood is soft, light colored, and is used for excelsior, woodenware, veneer core stock, and lumber. The tough inner bark was once used for rope. The leaves and fruits with the scaly wings were once used for a tea which had a medicinal value. This tea was used especially in Europe.

FROSTWEED

Helianthemum canadense (L.) Michx.
Rockrose Family

Frostweed at first has only one main stem with a flower at the top, but soon smaller, side branches will grow taller than the flower. It is a foot or more tall and has narrow, pointed, alternate leaves. The stem and leaves are hairy. The yellow flower has five large, overlapping petals and many stamens. It is about one inch across. Later in the season, clusters of flowers without petals appear on branches, are fertilized, but do not open. As fall approaches, the bark on the stem may split and release tiny strings of ice crystals, hence the name Frostweed.

GOLDEN HEATHER

Hudsonia ericoides L.
Rockrose Family

Golden Heather is a low, bushy plant which forms dense mats 1-8 inches high and up to two feet across. It grows in dry sandy soils in pine barrens and along the coast. The dry, brownish, hairy plant is very showy when in bloom. It has green spreading needle-like leaves which grow very close together on younger branches but are more scattered along older ones. Numerous vivid yellow blossoms terminate the short branches. The flowers are about ¼ inch across and have five notched petals. (In forma *leucantha*, the petals are white.)

WOOLLY HUDSONIA or
BEACH HEATHER

Hudsonia tomentosa Nutt.
Rockrose Family

This heather is a densely tufted or matted plant less than eight inches high. It usually grows on sand dunes along the coast, but is occasionally found inland in sandy areas. It is more common from southwestern Maine southward. It resembles Golden Heather, but the plant is grayer. The leaves are very close to the stem and the tips do not spread out. They are covered with a thin white wool. The flowers are at the tips of the leafy branches and may or may not have short stalks. Each flower has five sulphur-yellow petals.

LEATHERWOOD; MOOSEWOOD;
WICOPY

Dirca Palustris L.
Mezereum Family

Leatherwood is a much-branched shrub usually from 2-5 feet but occasionally up to 9 feet in height. It is rare throughout northern New England, but may be found in rich woods, thickets, moist ravines, and in near springs.

The alternate leaves are on very short stalks, and have no teeth on the margins. The leaves are dull light green, thin, broadly elliptical and up to three inches long. There is no tapering point, and the leaves are broadest at or above the middle.

The flowers are light yellow, in clusters of 3-4, and appear in April before the leaves. The fruit is a small, dull red, oval, berry-like drupe about ½ inch long. There is a single seed inside.

The shrub has a thick, gnarled, light dull brown trunk which is often in a leaning position. The short trunk divides into many curved branches just a short way up from the ground. The stems are soft and flexible but are very strong, with numerous, conspicuous swollen joints. The twigs are smooth, have a yellow green color, and are thickly clustered at the ends of the branches. Buds are hidden under the leaf stalk.

The wood is buff white and very flexible. The bark has been used medicinally as an emetic, and the fibrous bark was used by Indians for thongs.

buds hidden under leaf stem

actual size

DAPHNE
Daphne mezereum L.
Mezereum Family

Daphne is a shrub which is native to Europe but formerly was much planted here. It has escaped and become naturalized in overgrown fields and thickets, along old stonewalls, and by old lime quarries. It is an erect shrub 1-4 feet high with lilac-like flowers nearly ½ inch long which bloom before the leaves unfold. The funnel-shaped rose-purple to pink flowers have four overlapping, spreading lobes. The four golden-yellow anthers are attached on the inside of the calyx lobe, and can easily be seen protruding slightly from the throat of the flower. When mature, the leaves are 3-4 inches long and have toothless margins. The stems are stout and light brown. In spring they are often nubby with new leaf buds which have not opened yet. The flower clusters grow on shoots of the preceding year. The mature twigs may be nearly square or angular and more yellow-ocher in color than the new ones.

191

RUSSIAN OLIVE or OLEASTER
Elaeagnus angustifolia L.
Oleaster Family

Russian Olive is a shrub or small tree which is sometimes thorny and has silver branchlets. It is planted as an ornamental, but has occasionally escaped.

The alternate leaves are long and slender with a rounded tip and untoothed margins. The uppersurface is olive green, but the undersurface is white and almost silvery. Sometimes smaller leaves or branchlets grow from the axils of the leaves.

The fragrant flowers are in clusters of 1-3, on short stalks, and grow from the lower part of the branchlet. The flowers are yellow inside, but silvery on the outside. The olive-shaped fruit is yellow and coated with silvery scales. The flesh inside is sweet and mealy.

The twigs are silvery with a silver fuzz. New leaf buds form in the axils of the leaves.

SOAPBERRY or BUFFALO-BERRY
Shepherdia canadensis (L.) Nutt.
Oleaster Family

Soapberry is a thornless shrub 4-8 feet high which grows on banks along streams especially where there is limy soil. The young shoots are usually brown-scruffy. The elliptical leaves have untoothed margins. They may be green and hairless on the uppersurface, or may have a few silvery hairs. The underside has both silvery and rusty-brown scurf — some in the shape of stars. A hand lens will show the silvery cobweb-like hairs.

The inconspicuous pale yellow flowers are in short spikes at the nodes of the twigs. Male

1.

flowers are clustered, but female flowers are apt to be separate. The male flower has a four-part cupped calyx with 8 stamens protruding. The female flower has an urn-shaped calyx with four lobes at the tip. The disk on the tip of the protruding center nearly closes the opening. The fruit is red or yellowish and has a smooth pit inside.

Winter buds are clustered at nodes on the twigs. The terminal bud is paddle-shaped with a keel. It has two smaller buds at the base of it. The round flower buds are in clusters at the leaf nodes. The twig and the buds are both pitted with brown specks.

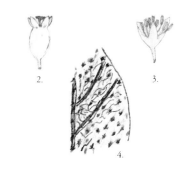

1. winter buds
2. enlarged female flower
3. enlarged male flower
4. enlarged scurf on under side of leaf

WATER WILLOW;
SWAMP LOOSESTRIFE;
WATER-OLEANDER
Decodon verticillatus (L.) Ell.
Loosestrife Family

Water Willow is a perennial herb or slightly-shrubby plant with arching branches. These arching branches may take root at the tips and start new plants. Water Willow grows in bogs, swamps, and edges of shallow ponds. It varies in height from 1 to 5 feet.

The slender leaves are lance-shaped and have little or no leaf stalks. They may be opposite on the stem or in whorls of three.

The pinkish to magenta flower has a cup-shaped calyx with from 5-7 erect, pointed teeth. The petals do not spread wide. There are ten stamens — of two different lengths — which protrude from the center of the petals. Flowers are in clusters at leaf axils.

The bark on the submersed part of the stem is thick and spongy. The stems above water are slightly hairy.

enlarged fruit

winter twig

with marginal fullness. The tip comes to an *abrupt point*.

Inconspicuous green flowers are in small clusters. Male and female flowers are *on different trees*. Fruit will only be on the trees that bear the female flowers. The long-stalked fruit is an oval, berry-like drupe which is blue-black when ripe. The fruits may be single or in clusters of 3 or 4 and each has a large stone inside. They ripen in September and October, and though they are bitter, many species of wildlife enjoy eating them.

The bark is deeply corrugated and gray on older trees. The *many short, horizontal or drooping branches* have smooth, light gray bark. The young twigs are greenish yellow at first. The leaf scars have three distinct bundle scars. The pith has regularly-spaced horizontal partitions.

The wood is heavy, soft, strong, tough and not durable. It is not commercially used in New England.

TUPELO; BLACK GUM; or SOUR GUM
Nyssa sylvatica Marsh.
Gum Family

Tupelo is only a medium-sized tree 20-50 feet tall in New England, but farther south it reaches heights to 100 feet. It is not common in New England, but is found occasionally from central Maine southward. Tupelo prefers wet ground and grows in and along borders of swamps, shores, and in low, acid woods.

The alternate leaves are rather leathery, 2-4 inches (3-10 cm.) long, and lustrous dark olive green on the uppersurface. The hairless leaves usually have toothless margins, but occasionally a leaf may have a few obscure teeth. The leaf blade may be egg-shaped, pointed at both ends, or have the broadest part above the middle. The edges may be ruffled

AMERICAN SPIKENARD
Aralia racemosa L.
Ginseng Family

American Spikenard is *not a shrub*, but because it grows to heights of 2-10 feet and a novice might call it a shrub and expect to find it in this book, it is included.

This large prickless-plant is very branching and grows in rich woods and thickets. It is known for its large, spicy, aromatic root. The slightly downy leaves are divided into three (rarely five) compound divisions. These divisions are then subdivided into thin heart-shaped leaflets with sharply-toothed margins and pointed tips. The greenish-white flowers

194

re in compound clusters along the main stem. The dark purple or reddish-brown fruit is a nearly round ridged berry enclosing five seeds. Other names given to this plant are Petty Morrel, Life-of-Man, Spice Bush, and Old Maid's Root.

HERCULES' CLUB or
ANGELICA TREE
Aralia spinosa L.
Ginseng Family

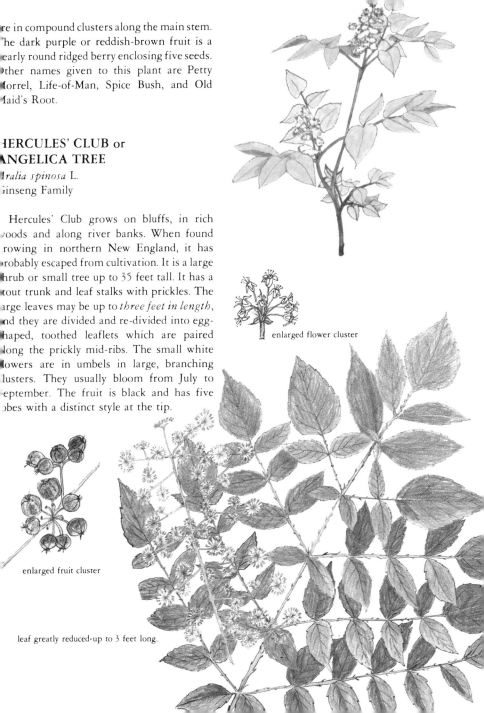

Hercules' Club grows on bluffs, in rich woods and along river banks. When found growing in northern New England, it has probably escaped from cultivation. It is a large shrub or small tree up to 35 feet tall. It has a stout trunk and leaf stalks with prickles. The large leaves may be up to *three feet in length*, and they are divided and re-divided into egg-shaped, toothed leaflets which are paired along the prickly mid-ribs. The small white flowers are in umbels in large, branching clusters. They usually bloom from July to September. The fruit is black and has five lobes with a distinct style at the tip.

enlarged flower cluster

enlarged fruit cluster

leaf greatly reduced-up to 3 feet long.

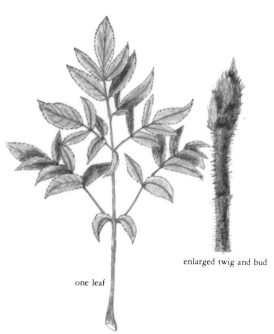

one leaf

enlarged twig and bud

BRISTLY SARSAPARILLA
Aralia hispida Vent.
Ginseng Family

Bristly Sarsaparilla is really a sub-shrub, for it is *woody at the base only*. The stem is very bristly with straight, stiff hairs. It grows in clearings and open woods, and along rocky and sandy railroad or road beds to heights of 1-3 feet.

The large leaves are divided and divided again into oblong-pointed leaflets with toothed margins. The leaflets may be entirely smooth or have hairs on the veins on the underside of the blade. The whitish flowers are arranged in several round umbels. These umbels are not on separate stalks, but several umbels are together on a single long stalk which extends above the leaves. The fruit is round and green when immature, but dark purple and strongly five-lobed when dry.

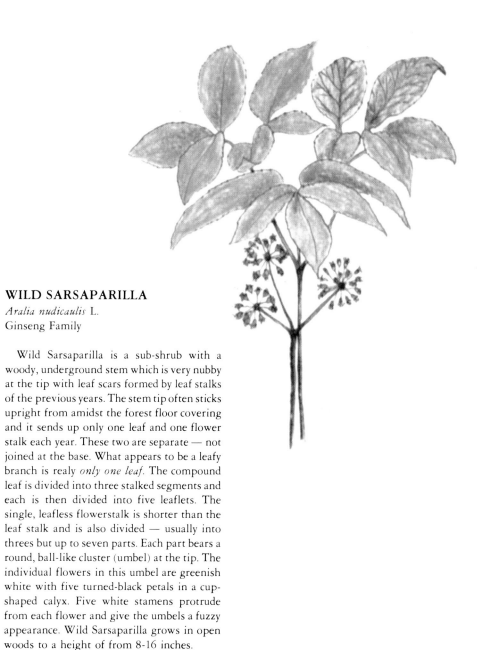

WILD SARSAPARILLA
Aralia nudicaulis L.
Ginseng Family

Wild Sarsaparilla is a sub-shrub with a woody, underground stem which is very nubby at the tip with leaf scars formed by leaf stalks of the previous years. The stem tip often sticks upright from amidst the forest floor covering and it sends up only one leaf and one flower stalk each year. These two are separate — not joined at the base. What appears to be a leafy branch is realy *only one leaf*. The compound leaf is divided into three stalked segments and each is then divided into five leaflets. The single, leafless flowerstalk is shorter than the leaf stalk and is also divided — usually into threes but up to seven parts. Each part bears a round, ball-like cluster (umbel) at the tip. The individual flowers in this umbel are greenish white with five turned-black petals in a cup-shaped calyx. Five white stamens protrude from each flower and give the umbels a fuzzy appearance. Wild Sarsaparilla grows in open woods to a height of from 8-16 inches.

FLOWERING DOGWOOD

Cornus florida L.
Dogwood Family

Here is a way to positively identify a dogwood. Hold a leaf between thumbs and forefingers so that the veins go across. Pull it apart gently. A thin white "web" will stretch between the ends of the broken veins. Viburnums — which some may confuse with dogwoods — will not produce this "web." This characteristic holds true in all dogwoods.

Flowering Dogwood is a small tree usually 15-25 feet tall, but it reaches heights up to 40 feet farther south. The trunk is rather straight up to the branches, and then it divides and branches until it disappears in the crown. It is uncommon in northern New England, (only one station in Maine) but is found in Massachusetts and southward. It prefers well-drained soil and is tolerant of shade. It is usually found under other trees in moist, fertile forests.

The dark green, opposite leaves are simple and clusterd towards the ends of the branches. They are 3-5 inches (8-13 cm.) long; have a pointed tip; have a base that is wedge-shaped; and have untoothed but *very wavy margins.* The midrib and curved veins are very prominent.

The flowers are not what they seem to be. The four broad, notched, petal-like divisions are really the bud scales of the flower bud. These scales winter over, and in the spring they grow out into large, white petal-like bracts. The real flowers are the greenish-white "dots" in the center.

The fruits are berry-like drupes born in a cluster. They are bright, shiny red, oval in shape, have a black tip, and contain a grooved stone.

The bark on older stems is like the skin of an alligator. It is reddish-brown to black and is broken up into four-sided scaly blocks. Bark on branches is light brown to reddish-gray. Branchlets are apt to be greenish.

The wood is valuable elsewhere, but it is not commercially used in New England. The beauty of the blossoming tree prevents most people in New England from cutting it down.

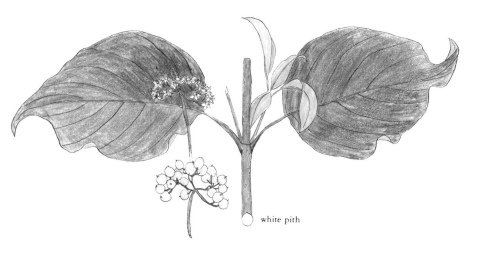

white pith

RED-OSIER DOGWOOD
Cornus stolonifera Michx.
Dogwood Family

Red-Osier Dogwood is a low, straggling shrub which reaches heights up to 9 feet, but is usually much shorter. The lower or underground shoots often take root and make new plants which form thickets or large clumps. It is common in northern New England — growing in moist soil along water — but is less common in the southern states.

The opposite leaves have toothless margins and are on short stalks — often with smaller branches growing from the leaf axils of larger leaves. The fine hairs on the upper surface of the leaf can be seen through a hand lens. The leaves are light olive green above and pale whitish underneath with conspicuous ribs.

The flowers are in flat-topped clusters about two inches across. Each flower has four dull, yellow-white petals. Flowers open in June. The fruit is usually dull white, but may be leaden gray or leaden blue. The size and shape of the fruit is variable. It may be longer than broad on some bushes, while being broader than long on the next bush; while fruit on a third bush may be black dotted. The fruit is in ruddy-stemmed clusters which mature in August.

The bush has smooth, bright crimson twigs and shoots which are scattered with wart-like grayish or whitish dots. Bark on larger stems is smooth and brownish tan in color.

ROUND-LEAVED DOGWOOD
Cornus rugosa Lam.
Dogwood Family

    This dogwood is a coarse shrub up to 10 feet in height which grows in well drained woods and rocky sopes, usually where it is shady. The opposite leaves are broadly-oval or nearly round — sometimes even wider than they are long. The leaf has *7 or more pairs of prominent veins* while other dogwoods usually have six or less.

    The small white flowers are in flat-topped clusters on stout, somewhat hairy stalks. The clusters may be as wide as three inches, and they usually open in June. The fruit is light blue — rarely white — with a nearly round, ridged stone inside. The branches are rather warty and are *greenish with purple blotches.* The pith inside is white.

See note on p. 198 for a clue to identification.

SILKY CORNEL; KINNIKINICK; SWAMP or SILKY DOGWOOD
Cornus amomum Mill.
Dogwood Family

    Silky Dogwood is a loosely-spreading shrub 3 to 10 feet in height. It resembles Red-Osier Dogwood, but the stems are reddish-brown — *not deep red.* It is common in New England on shores of ponds, along streams and rivers, and in moist thickets.

    The large, light olive green leaves have a rounded base and abruptly come to a sharp-pointed tip. The leaves may be from 3-4 inches (7-10 cm.) long and have gray or rusty hairs on the underside.

    The white flowers are in compact, flat-topped clusters 1½ to 2½ inches (4-7 cm.) across. The stalks of the flower clusters are covered with silky hairs. The flowers bloom in June, and each one has a cup-shaped calyx with four long, narrow petals.

The fruit is dull or light blue to lead colored and is about ¼ inch (5-8 mm.) in diameter. Each berry-like drupe contains a narrow, ridged stone which is pointed at the base.

The bark is smooth and streaked. On older branches it is dark, ocher brown but newer twigs are maroon to purplish and are *covered with gray silky hairs*. The pith inside is brown and drab.

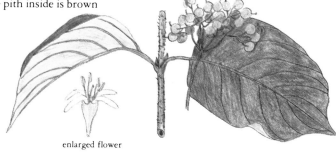

enlarged flower

PALE or SILKY DOGWOOD
Cornus obliqua Raf.
Dogwood Family

C. obliqua is similar to *C. amomum* and is often confused with it. This dogwood grows in swamps and damp thickets, and the brown stems have gray fuzz — especially at the axils of the leaves. *C. obliqua* differs mostly in the leaves. The leaves are narrower and have tapering (or wedge-shaped) bases and gradually tapering points. The upper surface is olive green, but the lower surface has appressed white hairs or is covered with a whitish waxy coating which can be rubbed off. The leaf blades on fertile branchlets are ½ to 2 inches (1.5-2 cm.) broad and on the average are *less than half as broad as long*.

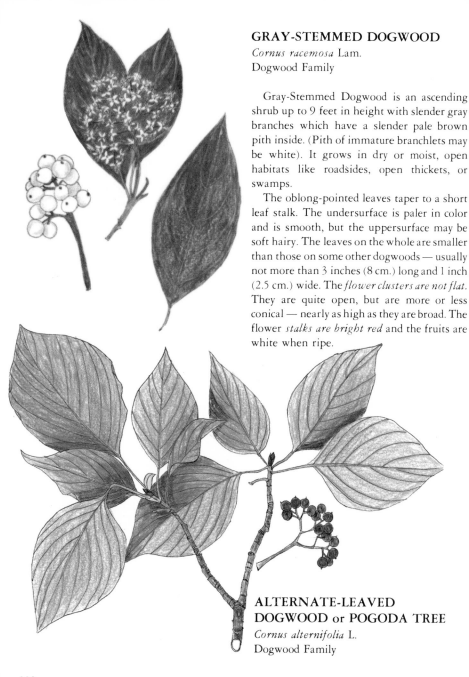

GRAY-STEMMED DOGWOOD

Cornus racemosa Lam.
Dogwood Family

Gray-Stemmed Dogwood is an ascending shrub up to 9 feet in height with slender gray branches which have a slender pale brown pith inside. (Pith of immature branchlets may be white). It grows in dry or moist, open habitats like roadsides, open thickets, or swamps.

The oblong-pointed leaves taper to a short leaf stalk. The undersurface is paler in color and is smooth, but the uppersurface may be soft hairy. The leaves on the whole are smaller than those on some other dogwoods — usually not more than 3 inches (8 cm.) long and 1 inch (2.5 cm.) wide. The *flower clusters are not flat.* They are quite open, but are more or less conical — nearly as high as they are broad. The flower *stalks are bright red* and the fruits are white when ripe.

ALTERNATE-LEAVED DOGWOOD or POGODA TREE

Cornus alternifolia L.
Dogwood Family

Alternate-Leaved Dogwood is a shrub or a small tree up to 20 feet in height with a broad, flattened crown. Both the branches and the leaves are in flat layers which are a characteristic of this dogwood. It grows in well-drained woodlands.

The alternate leaves tend to be crowded at the tips of the branchlets. They have very prominent curved veins, are from 2½ to 4½ inches long, and taper to slender stalks at the base. The uppersurface is yellowish green and smooth, while the lowersurface may have fine hairs pressed close to it.

Small, creamy-white flowers appear in June after the leaves have developed. These are arranged in loose, flat-topped clusters rather than in heads. The fruit is a bluish-black, nearly-round drupe which ripens in September and October.

Bark of young trees is smooth and dark reddish-brown; on older trees it is fissured. The twigs are often lustrous greenish brown, but become bright yellow-green when they die. Twigs on older trees have lines encircling them and the old leaf scars are very conspicuous.

SWEET PEPPERBUSH
Clethra alnifolia L.
White Alder Family

Sweet Pepperbush is a shrub from 3-10 feet tall which grows in wet places and often forms large thickets. It is occasionally found in wet woods. It is one of the few plants to produce side growth from the new shoots. The deep green leaves are 1-3 inches (3.5-7 cm.) long. The widest part of the leaf is above the middle. The leaf blade is *untoothed towards the base* but the outer part is toothed. The veins are straight and prominent. Both surfaces of the leaf are smooth and green. The flowers are very fragrant with a *spicy odor.* They have five white petals and a long protruding pistil in the center. (There is a form *rosea* where the petals are a rosy pink.) The spherical fruit is a three-part capsule. The slender stems have dull, dark brown bark and the young twigs are covered with minute gray hairs.

enlarged fruit

PIPSISSEWA or PRINCE'S PINE
Chimaphila umbellata
var. *cisatlantica* (L.) Blake
Wintergreen Family

This rather woody plant is borderline between a shrub and an herb, but is here included with the other woody plants. Pipsissewa grows in great patches on the floor of forests where there is an underlying sandy soil and a carpet of decaying leaves or pine needles. The plant grows to a height of from 4-12 inches.

Numerous shiny evergreen leaves are arranged in whorls or scattered along the stem. The leaves vary in length from 1-2½ inches, (3-7 cm.) are sharply toothed at the margins, and may have blunt or pointed tips. The flowers — arranged in a loose cluster at the tip of a long stalk — are about ½ inch (1-2 cm.) broad and vary in color from white to dark pink. The five petals are decidedly cup-shaped, rounded at the tips, and spread open. Ten violet anthers are evenly arranged like beads around the flat-topped central pistil. The fruiting body is a dry, brown capsule. There is a dark brown — almost black — round disk in the center and the capsule splits into five parts from the tip to the base. These fruits usually remain on the plant all winter.

enlarged fruit

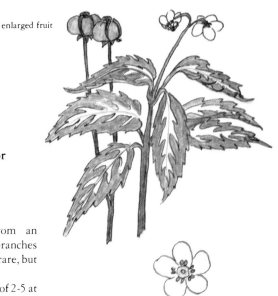

enlarged flower

SPOTTED WINTERGREEN or SPOTTED PIPSISSEWA

Chimaphila maculata (L.) Pursh
Wintergreen Family

This woodland plant grows from an underground stem and has erect branches from four to ten inches tall. They are rare, but can be found in dry woods.

The nodding flowers are in clusters of 2-5 at the tips of erect flower stalks. The waxy flowers are very fragrant and may be white or tinged with pink. They have five petals and ten stamens which form a crown in the center. The round tip of the pistil (stigma) forms the central point of the crown. The long evergreen leaves are arranged in whorls of four or may be scattered on the stem. They are sharply pointed, toothed, and have a very beautiful white variegation at the center along the veins.

LABRADOR TEA

Ledum groenlandicum Oeder
Heath Family

Labrador Tea is a northern evergreen shrub which grows in cold, wet bogs, moist thickets, and peaty soils to a height of 1-3½ feet. It has brown twigs, and newer twigs are extremely velvet-hairy with rust-colored hairs. The leathery, narrow, toothless leaves have rolled-under edges and rusty-brown wool on the underside of the leaves. Newer leaves may have white instead of orange wool. The leaves are fragrant when crushed and have been used for a tea.

The creamy white flowers are in clusters at the ends of the twigs. Each cluster has twelve or more flowers — each on a long, downy flower stalk. At the base of these stalks are cupped, rusty-colored bracts which become loose and fall off. The five white stamens protruding from each flower give the cluster a feathery look from a distance. Each flower is about 1/3 inch (8-10 mm.) broad and has five spreading petals, a small five-toothed green calyx, and a green ovary in the center.

The solid, elliptical capsule is about ¼ inch long and *opens from the base upwards*. These nodding capsules are in clusters which remain on the shrub through the winter.

RHODODENDRON;
GREAT LAUREL; ROSE BAY
Rhododendron maximum L.
Heath Family

Rhododendron is a large shrub or straggling tree up to 25 or 30 feet in height. Sometimes many trees grow together and their branches interlace and form almost impenetrable rhododendron jungles. It grows on shaded rocky slopes and in damp woods or swamps, but it is very rare in northern New England. Rhododendron was *protected by law in Maine.*

The large, thick, leathery leaves may be as long as 10 inches (.8-2.5 dm.). They are alternate, but are mostly clustered at the tips of the branchlets. The leaves are evergreen and are usually covered with a fine wool on the lower surface.

The pink or white waxy flowers are in large, showy clusters. A single flower is somewhat bell-shaped, but has five spreading petals. The flower is greenish in the throat, and may have red, yellow, or green spots on the upper surface of the petals. The calyx is very small and has five pointed sepals.

The fruit is a dry pod about ½ inch (1-1.5 cm.) long. The tip splits into five parts and the long slender style protrudes from the center. The fruit capsules remain on the tree until the following season.

The bark is thin reddish-brown, and — on older trees — peels off in thin scales. New twigs are green and coated with rusty hair at first, but later become smooth and reddish-brown. The cone-shaped leaf buds form in mid-summer in the axils of the leaves. The flower buds form at the tips of the branchlets. These are 1-1½ inches (2.5-4 cm.) long and are covered with numerous overlapping, green bracts.

greatly reduced

LAPLAND RHODODENDRON
Rhododendron lapponicum (L.) Wahlenb.
Heath Family

This is a dwarf rhododendron which grows in higher elevations of New England and New York. It is a freely branching shrub, not much taller than a foot. The leaves are less than an inch long. The leaves are oval, leathery, evergreen, and scaly on the underside. The bright purple flowers are in small clusters at the ends of the branches — usually only two or three in a cluster. Each flower is less than three-fourths of an inch broad. The pistils and stamens are very noticeable.

RHODORA
Rhododendron canadense (L.) Torr.
Heath Family

Rhodora is an erect northern shrub that grows best in cold, wet, acid, or peaty soil in the full sun. It often grows in large colonies in old pastures. It is usually from 1-3 feet tall and has many branches and showy clusters of two-lipped flowers which bloom in late May — usually before the leaves unfold.

The oval leaves are green on top and lighter underneath. New growth in summer may be gray or blue-green. The leaves have untoothed margins, but there may be a sharp point at the tip. The *leaves are not evergreen* and are usually hairy underneath — at least at the midvein.

The conspicuous rose-purple flowers are about ½ inch wide and up to 1½ inches long. The lower lip is divided into two long narrow petals and the upper lip is upright and three-parted. Ten showy stamens protrude from the throat of the flower. They are about as long as the petals. The fruit cluster is made up of 3-5 thick, curved capsules — usually pale pink or lavender in color. The drying style remains attached to the tip. The sides of the capsule are somewhat ribbed and are noticeably hairy. Some hairs are tipped with glands.

PINXTER FLOWER
Rhododendron nudiflorum (L.) Torr.
Heath Family

Pinxter Flower is a shrub which grows in rocky woods, thickets and swamps to heights of 2-6 feet. The flower opens before the leaves expand. The leaves are green on both sides and are extremely variable in size, shape, and texture. The leaves may be elliptical, may have the greatest width above the middle, or may come abruptly to a point. Usually the underside is slightly hairy, especially along the midrib and on the leaf stalk. The funnel-shaped flowers may be flesh-color or pale pink but they are deep ruddy pink or magenta at the base on the outside. Usually they are odorless. The long stamens and the pistil protrude from the throat of the flower. The calyx lobes and the outside of the flower have fine hairs on them.

EARLY AZALEA or ELECTION PINK or HONEYSUCKLE

Rhododendron roseum (Loisel.) Rehd.
Heath Family

Early Azalea is a shrub which grows to heights up to 9 feet in dry woods, thickets, and rocky banks. It is uncommon in Maine, New Hampshire, and Vermont, but when introduced it has survived. This azalea becomes more common in southern New England.

The leaves are 1-4 inches long and are arranged in rosettes at the tips of the twigs. They are oval with slight points at both ends and are hairy on the under surface, especially at the margins. The twigs may be roughened with gray hairiness. The showy, *very fragrant flowers* are in clusters at the tips of the twigs. The blossom may be 1½ to 2 inches long and blooms in June. The tubular flowers have five spreading lobes which twist and fold along the margins or at the tip. The five red stamens are about twice the length of the corolla tube and protrude in a graceful curve. The throat of the flower about equals the length of the petal and is hairy both on the outside and the inside. When the petals and stamens fall, the long curved style remains attached to the hairy green ovary. The mature fruit pod is more than ½ inch long and splits into five parts.

CLAMMY AZALEA; SWAMP HONEYSUCKLE; or SWAMP PINK

Rhododendron viscosum (L.) Torr.
Heath Family

Clammy Azalea is a branching shrub 3-8 feet high which usually has many, hairy, light

rown branches and twigs. It grows in
wamps, thickets, and damp clearings —
sually near the coast — from Maine
outhward.

The leaves have a narrow base and are
sually *widest above the middle*. They are 1-4
nches (2-10 cm.) long and are on very short
talks. They are usually glossy green on both
ides, but on some leaves the underside may be
ecidedly whitened. There are hairs at the
eins on the underside of the leaf. Often the
eaves are arranged in clusters at the tips of the
wigs.

The fragrant funnel-shaped flowers bloom
n early summer when the leaves are fully
rown. The sticky, hairy *tube is much longer
han the five spreading lobes*. The flowers are
sually white, but may be pale pink or white
ith pink stripes on the outside of the lobes.

reduced plant

ALPINE AZALEA

oiseleuria procumbens (L.) Desv.
Heath Family

This azalea is a much-branched, spreading,
ather matted, dwarf shrub which only grows
n the summits of our taller mountains. The
hort, leafy branches may be only 2-5 inches
ng on some matted plants.

The minute, evergreen leaves are usually
pposite, but are crowded on the stems. They
re rarely more than 1/3 of an inch (1 cm.)
ng and have short leaf stalks. They are dark
vergreen above, paler below, with a *very
rominent midrib on the underside*. The
argins are turned under.

The tiny, bell-shaped flowers have five
bes and are in terminal clusters of 2-5
owers. They may be deep crimson pink or
hite. The cup-shaped calyx is almost as long
s the cup-shaped corolla.

greatly enlarged leaf

reduced plant

MOUNTAIN LAUREL
Kalmia latifolia L.
Heath Family

Mountain Laurel is a large shrub which grows to 20 feet tall farther south. It has stout, forking or inclining stems with divergent branches which form a round, compact head. It grows in rocky or gravelly woods and clearings, and sometimes in swamps; it is rare in northern New England and was *protected by law in Maine*. It is the state flower of Connecticut.

The alternate — sometimes paired — leaves are dark green and glossy on the top and yellow-green underneath. They have a wedge-shaped base, a pointed tip, and untoothed margins. Sometimes the leaf is tipped with a bristle point. Leaves are from 3-4 inches in length. Mature leaves are thick and leathery and will remain on a tree for two seasons.

Flower buds are pointed and scalloped around the base and are very attractive. The flowers are saucer-shaped with five short, pointed lobes. Each is on a red or green hairy stalk in dense, showy, terminal clusters. They vary in color from white, to pink-tinged, to pink or rose, and open at the end of June or in early July — earlier farther south. There are ten arching stamens which are embedded in depressions on the inside rim of the flower.

The fruit is round in outline, but is slightly five-lobed and covered with hairs. Both the style and the calyx remain on the fruit.

The bark is very thin, reddish-brown, furrowed, and peels off in long, narrow, thin scales to expose the cinnamon-red inner bark. Winter buds are alternate, sharp-pointed, and greenish in color.

The wood is heavy, hard, strong, and brittle. It would make excellent fuel if it were more plentiful. In New England, the wood is not commercially used.

SHEEP LAUREL or LAMBKILL
Kalmia angustifolia L.
Heath Family

Sheep Laurel is a small slender shrub usually less than three feet tall. It has straight ascending stems. The older leaves usually hang downward; the flower cluster develops above the old leaves; and new leaves rise from amidst the flower cluster. Sheep Laurel is common throughout northern New England in moist open places in swamps, bogs, pastures, and on rocky slopes. The plants are poisonous to livestock.

The evergreen leaves — usually in whorls of three — are smooth, rather shiny, and crowded on the branches. The elliptical leathery leaves have rounded tips and short stalks, and are deep green above and paler beneath.

The deep pink, saucer-shaped flowers are from ¼ to ½ inch accross. The stamens are arranged like spokes of a wheel, and the tip of each is embedded in a depression at the rim of the corolla. The fruits are round pods containing many small seeds. These fruits remain on the plants all winter. The branches are round and hairless.

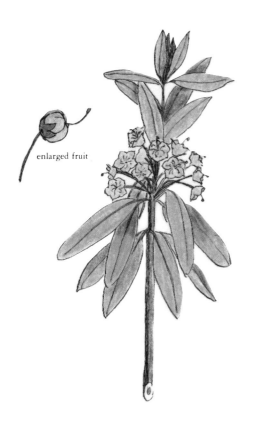

enlarged fruit

BOG or PALE LAUREL
Kalmia polifolia Wang.
Heath Family

Bog Laurel is a small shrub found in bogs — it is usually less than three feet tall. It is sparingly branched and has leaves which are arranged in pairs and are ½-2 inches long. The edges of the leaves are rolled backwards and the undersides of the leaves are covered with white hairs. The flowers are similar to those of Mountain Laurel but are smaller and paler in color.

213

MOUNTAIN HEATH
Phyllodoce coerulea (L.) Bab.
Heath Family

Mountain Heath is a low (4-6 inches) alpine evergreen shrub. The branches are crowded with linear leaves which have rough margins. Mountain Heath grows in alpine areas of the summits of higher mountains in New England. The Latin name *coerulea* is not a good choice, for it means sky-blue. This flower is never bluish in America — unless perhaps when it is going by. The flowers are light lavender to purple, are barrel-shaped, have five lobes at the tip, and are about ⅜ inch (7-8 mm.) in length. The flowers nod from erect flower stalks at the summit of the branches. The calyx is hairy, and the style does not protrude. The fruit capsule has five valves and contains many seeds. The flower stalks elongate as the flower goes to seed. The remnants of the pistil remain on the tip of the seed capsule.

BOG ROSEMARY
Andromeda glaucophylla Link.
Heath Family

Bog Rosemary is a low evergreen shrub of northern New England. It grows in bogs, peaty marshes, and margins of ponds to a height of from one to three feet. It may cover great patches in a bog. The shrub does not have many branches, but many shrubs will grow together to form a clump. The leaves on new growth are usually longer — up to 2½ inches (6-7 cm.) — than leaves on older shrubs. Firm, narrow leaves are alternate on the woody stem. They are blue-green on the top, covered with short white hairs on the underside, and have margins which *roll under*. The bell-shaped, nodding flowers are ¼ inch long and may be white, pink, or white tinged with crimson. Each flower is on its own curved pedicel (flower stalk), but several flowers occur together in a curved umbel at the tip of a branch. The dry fruit has five divisions and resembles a small brown pumpkin. These fruits may stay on the plant all winter.

MALEBERRY
Lyonia ligustrina (L.) DC.
Heath Family

Maleberry is an erect shrub which may reach heights of ten feet, but is most commonly five or six feet tall. It grows in swampy woods, edges of ponds or swamps, and in thickets.

The leaves are about two inches long and are broadest at or above the middle. They have a short point at the tip and may be toothless or have finely-toothed margins. The thick leaves are scurfy on the upper surface and are poisonous to young stock.

The flowers are in one-sided racemes containing as many as 50 flowers. The individual flowers are urn-shaped with recurved teeth at the tip.

The fruit is a dry, yellow-brown capsule which splits and divides into five distinct parts. These turn brown and remain on the plant all winter. The capsules may be hairy.

The bark is light colored with loose, shedding bark. The crimson-colored buds are smooth, slender and sharp-pointed. Each bud has two scales and is flattened very close to the twig.

LEATHERLEAF or CASSANDRA

Chamaedaphne calyculata L. var. *angustifolia* (Ait.) Rehd.
Heath Family

Leatherleaf is a profusely-branching shrub which grows in bogs, swales, and borders of shallow ponds or lakes. It seldom gets taller than three feet.

The elliptical, leathery-textured leaves are dull green — almost evergreen in fact. They have cinnamon brown scales on the underside. Large leaves are usually from 1-1½ inches long and leaves *get progressively smaller* as they near the tip of the branch. Leaves are usually not very pointed and the margins may or may not have very fine, indistinct teeth.

The delicate bell-shaped white flowers are in *one-sided leafy racemes* at the tips of tough, wiry branches. The flowers are suspended on tiny stalks from the base of small, upturned leaves, and open in May. The calyx has five distinct, pointed sepals which remain on the fruit. The capsule is depressed, has five parts, and contains many flattened seeds.

MOSS PLANT or CASSIOPE

Cassiope hypnoides (L.) D. Don
Heath Family

Cassiope is a low heath-like shrub which is much-branched, tufted, or moss-like. It grows in small trailing colonies in mossy alpine areas of mountain summits, but it *is very rare*. Cassiope seldom reaches a height of more than four inches (1-12 cm.).

The slender, evergreen needle-like leaves overlap each other on the stem. Solitary bell or cup-shaped flowers nod from the tips of the branches. The flowers are white or tinged with rose. There are *four red sepals* which form a cross at the base of the flower cup. The corolla is five-clefted and has eight or ten stamens in the center. The fruit is a small round pod.

TRAILING ARBUTUS or MAYFLOWER
Epigaea repens L.
Heath Family

Trailing Arbutus is a dwarf, creeping shrub which is seldom over 3 inches in height. It is a slow-growing shrub which thrives in sandy soil and partial shade. If you must have a slip of this plant in the spring, *do not pull it up*. Snip the flower-bearing tips and let the woody stem remain. Mayflower is on most conservation lists and should not be picked unless absolutely necessary.

The leaves are from 1-2 inches (2-5 cm.) long and have brownish hairs on the underside. Leaves are rounded, have a heart-shaped base and have rust-colored hairs on the leaf stalk. Flower buds are formed in the fall, and they open in early April or May soon after the snow melts. The fragrant, exquisite waxy flower clusters are partially hidden by the round-textured leaves of the previous year. Individual flowers are tubular with five spreading lobes and a fringe of hairs in the slender throat. There are 10 stamens. The woody stem has rusty hairs. The fruit is a somewhat depressed, fleshy capsule which becomes dry in age.

CHECKERBERRY or WINTERGREEN
Gaultheria procumbens L.
Heath Family

    Wintergreen is a low, spicy, semi-woody plant with creeping roots and underground stems. The branches are erect and upright and stand from two to six inches tall. Each stem bears several thick, oblong evergreen leaves that are shiny on top and pale underneath. The flowers are white or sometimes touched with pink. They are bell-shaped and hang down from the curved stalk. They are found in woods and open places in sandy soil — especially near evergreen trees. The fruit is a bright red berry and often lasts throughout the winter until the new blossoms appear in the spring.

CREEPING SNOWBERRY
Gaultheria hispidula (L.) Bigel.
Heath Family

    Creeping Snowberry is a delicate, trailing, matted evergreen with barely-woody stems. It grows in mossy woods and cold bogs — often at higher elevations where it tends to form mats. Creeping stems may be 3 to 12 inches long.
    The tiny oval leaves are stalked and have pointed tips. The upper surface is smooth and dark green, but the lower surface is yellow-green with rather long, stiff, brown hairs which can be seen with the naked eye. The margins are rolled under and are hairy. New leaves are apt to be yellow-green in color.
    There are only a few solitary blossoms which nod from the leaf axils. These tiny

white bell-shaped flowers are hidden beneath the leaves. The corolla is deeply cut into 4 parts. There are eight stamens inserted on an 8-toothed disk.

The fruit is a bright, white, juicy berry with a wintergreen flavor. It is usually minutely bristly and is topped with four calyx teeth. The fleshy calyx at the base enlarges as the berry matures.

The slender woody branches are brown with long brownish hairs. The newer growth is yellow green and is fuzzy with silvery hairs.

BEARBERRY

Arctostaphylos uva-ursi (L.) Spreng.
    var. *coactilis* Fern. & Macbr.
Heath Family

Bearberry is a trailing shrub with paddle-shaped leaves on flexible branches. The bark is papery, a reddish to ashy color, and peels readily. Bearberry forms dense carpets several yards wide and less than 6 inches (1½ dm.) high in dry sandy banks, and on shores, open rocky slopes and ledges. It is sometimes planted as a ground cover by highway departments. The numerous, opposite, small, leathery leaves are shiny and evergreen. Each twig tip appears to end in a rosette of leaves. The small, waxy white flowers hang in clusters of from 5-12 from the tips of the branch. Each flower is urn-shaped, about ¼ inch (5 mm.) long, with a small, lobed mouth which may be tinged with pink. The flowers open in May. The fruit is a dull, dry, berry-like drupe with a single stone. It ripens in July but lasts into November. Other names for this plant are Kinnikinick, Mealberry, Hog-Cranberry and Bousserole.

ALPINE or BLACK BEARBERRY
Arctostaphylos alpina (L.) Spreng.
Heath Family

Alpine Bearberry is a matted or prostrate shrub 2-5 inches tall which grows on bare rock and gravel in arctic-alpine regions of Mt. Katahdin in Maine and on some of the higher mountains of New Hampshire. It has dark-colored, brittle branches which are covered with papery bark. The leaves are long and narrow with the widest part being near the tip, and the base narrowing gradually to a long, slender stalk with bristles. The leaf has a wrinkled or leather-like appearance and the veins form an intricate and prominent network. The margin of the leaf is only toothed around the broad tip. The leaves will wither in winter and turn whitish with age, but will remain on the shrub. The flowers — only a few at the tip of each branch — will appear from scaly buds before or with the new leaves. The corolla is urn-shaped and constricted at the throat. It is whitish with five green lobes. There are 10 stamens, but they do not protrude from the throat of the flower. The fruit is a juicy, edible, purple or purple-black drupe.

enlarged flower   enlarged leaf

HEATHER or
SCOTCH HEATHER
Calluna vulgaris (L.) Hall
Heath Family

Heather is a low fern-like evergreen shrub with tiny, sharp, needle-like leaves in four rows along the branches. It was introduced from Europe, but has now become naturalized in peaty or damp sandy soils. This shrub is from five to fifteen inches tall. Minute opposite leaves are crowded and overlap each other on the branches. The flowers are usually purplish, but are pink on horticultural varieties. The flowers are in long — sometimes one-sided — clusters at the tips of the branches. The corolla is much shorter and is less showy than the calyx of four colored sepals. (See enlargement.)

CROSS-LEAVED HEATHER
Erica tetralix L.
Heath Family

Cross-Leaved Heather is a low, much-branded, straggling shrub with tiny *leaves in whorls of four* at regular intervals on the erect branches. This heather is an introduced plant but has been located in Franklin County, Maine, and in a few places on Cape Cod and Nantucket Island in Massachusetts. It seldom grows taller than four or five inches and grows in peaty clearings, open woods, and margins of bogs. The tiny leaves are stalked and have rolled-under margins. When looked at under a hand lens, the leaves are very fuzzy with short white hairs and long gland-tipped hairs at regular intervals along the margins. The tan stem is also covered with fuzzy white hairs. At the tips of the erect branches is a cluster of several barrel-shaped, deep pink flowers with four very hairy sepals. The flowers are about ¼ inch (6-8 mm.) and have four lobes at the tips.

1. enlarged flower
2. enlarged lower surface of leaf

enlarged
flower

DWARF HUCKLEBERRY
Gaylussacia dumosa (Andr.) T. & G.
  var. *bigeloviana* Fern.
Heath Family

Dwarf Huckleberry grows in sphagnous bogs and in wet peat and is much less common than Black Huckleberry. It is a low shrub 4-20 inches (1-5 dm.) in height. It has slender, somewhat glandular-hairy branches which rise from a creeping, underground base. The alternate leaves are narrow and wedge-shaped with a conspicuous point at the tip. A hand lens will show the orange, gland-tipped hairs *on both surfaces* on the leaf. These hairs are especially noticeable along the leaf margins. The uppersurface of the leaves is a lustrous olive-green. The bell-shaped flowers are white or pink and are arranged in a loose cluster on a slender, leafy stalk. They bloom in July and August and are less than ½ inch (8-9 mm.) long. The berry-like drupe is black when ripe and has glandular hairs on it. There are ten one-seeded nutlets inside. The immature fruit is hard and green with five red sepals. The fruit on this plant is not tasty as is that on the Black Huckleberry.

DANGLEBERRY or HUCKLEBERRY
Gaylussacia frondosa (L.) T. & G.
Heath Family

Dangleberry is a slender shrub up to 6 feet in height which grows in dry sandy woods and clearings from southern New Hampshire southward. Young branchlets are smooth or minutely hairy. The rather large, oval leaves are up to three inches long. They are yellow-green on the top and have fine hairs and a whitish covering beneath. There are small, inconspicuous resin dots on the lower surface only. Barrel-shaped flowers are in loose, leafy-bracted clusters up to three inches long. The corolla may be pinkish or greenish, and the *stamens do not protrude*. The flower stalks are longer than the flowers. The fruit is a dark-blue, berry-like drupe with a pale bloom. It is sweet and juicy, but contains 10 seed-like nutlets.

BLACK HUCKLEBERRY or HIGH-BUSH HUCKLEBERRY

Gaylussacia baccata (Michx.) Gray
Heath Family

Huckleberry is an erect shrub with many stiff gray-brown branches containing many leaves. The bush grows to heights of 1-3 feet on ledges; in dry or wet open woods and thickets; and especially by the edges of ponds and bogs. It is common in southern and central Maine, New Hampshire, and Vermont, but becomes less common farther north.

The small, oval leaves have pointed tips and toothless margins and are usually less than 1½ inches (2-4 cm.) long. They are densely covered on both sides with shiny resin globules which are sticky when the leaves are young. Buds also have resin globules on them.

The flowers are nearly cylindrical or urn-shaped with an open tip. They are greenish, tinged with crimson. Flowers are arranged in short, one-sided clusters amid ruddy-colored bracts.

The fruit is usually a shiny black, but may be dark blue with a bloom. It is edible and sweet, but contains 10 rather large seeds (nutlets) inside. The berry matures in August and is about ¼ inch in diameter.

reduced

1.

2.

1. enlarged bud showing resin globules
2. enlarged flower

enlarged flowers

DEERBERRY or SQUAW-HUCKLEBERRY
Vaccinium stamineum L.
Heath Family

Deerberry is a low branching shrub which is usually less than five feet tall, but occasionally reaches heights up to 10 feet (.3-3m.). It grows in dry woods, thickets and clearings but is only found in southern New England. The young branchlets are green or buff-colored and are downy. The leaves are 2-3½ inches (5-9 cm.) and are hairy and whitened on the lower surface. The top surface of the leaf is dull and is not shiny or hairy. Numerous flowers are in graceful, loose, leafy-bracted clusters. Each flower is on its own thread-like stalk which is jointed to the bract below it. The caylx has five teeth. The corolla is greenish-white to purple, but turns black as it dries. It is barrel-shaped with an open tip and five spreading lobes. Ten stamens protrude from the opening. The tough-skinned berry is juicy and contains soft seeds. It may be round or rather pear-shaped. It may be amber, purple, or blue in color, and may or may not have a bloom. The berry is not edible, and drops soon after it ripens.

BOG or ALPINE BILBERRY
Vaccinium uliginosum L.
Heath Family

Bog Bilberry is a deciduous low or prostrate branching plant which grows in dry, peaty barrens and on mountain summits of New England. The thick, dull-green or bluish green leaves are very leathery. They may be oblong or nearly round, have untoothed margins, and are pale and finely veined on the underside. The twigs are stout and nubby, and the branches are woody and strong. The tiny white or pinkish-tinged flowers are hollow and cylindrical with 4 petal-like lips at the tip. Each flower is on a short, curved stalk which originates from the leaf axil. The sweet, edible fruit is blue or black with a bloom.

enlarged flower

DWARF BILBERRY
Vaccinium caespitosum Michx.
Heath Family

Dwarf Bilberry is similar to the one above, except that the leaves are narrow or spatulate shaped with the widest part at or above the middle. They are smooth and shining (not dull as is Bog Bilberry) and have *tiny teeth on the margins*. This plant has tufted branches. The solitary flowers in the leaf axils *have five petal-like tips* instead of four. These flowers nod from short flower stalks and the corolla is deep pink to coral reddish. The berries are light blue with a bloom. Dwarf Bilberry grows on gravelly or rocky shores and openings in woods, both in alpine areas and at sea level.

leaves   enlarged flower and petals

225

SOUR TOP or
VELVETLEAF BLUEBERRY
Vaccinium myrtilloides Michx.
Heath Family

This blueberry is a low shrub usually not more than 1 foot high. It is common throughout northern and central Maine, New Hampshire and Vermont, but becomes less common farther south. It grows in moist to dry open woods, on ledges, and up to altitudes of 4000 feet, but it does not grow in alpine areas. The hairiness on this plant is very noticeable on the leaves and especially on the new young twigs.

The leaves are toothless and about 1 inch long. They are finely hairy or velvety beneath and often on the top surface as well. The flowers are greenish or may be tinged with purple. They are in clusters which appear in May when the leaves are half grown. The berries are rather large and are more sour than *V. vacillans* and *V. angustifolium* but they are edible. They are blue with a heavy bloom and ripen in late July.

EARLY LOWBUSH BLUEBERRY;
LOW BLUEBERRY;
EARLY SWEET BLUEBERRY
Vaccinium vacillans Torr.
Heath Family

This blueberry is a low shrub up to 2½ feet high (3-9 dm.) with stiff greenish or brown-tinged branches. It grows in dry open woods, warm rocky slopes, or clearings. The *leathery leaves* are larger than on the other low blueberries shown in this book. They may be

226

1-2 inches (1.5-5 cm.) long and are usually without teeth, but may have a few small teeth towards the tip. The leaves are dull and pale on top with a prominent network of veins, and are even paler below. The greenish-purple or purplish flowers are in racemes at the tips of branches. The calyx is often reddish. The plants bloom when leaves are only partly grown. The berries are dark blue with a faint bloom. They are sweet and have a good flavor.

LATE SWEET or
LOW SWEET BLUEBERRY
Vaccinium angustifolium Ait.
Heath Family

This blueberry is a low branching shrub which varies in height from 6 inches to 2 feet (.5-3.5 dm.). It spreads by means of underground stems. It usually grows in dry open barrens or sandy, rocky soil, but also grows in bogs and in alpine areas.

The leaves vary in size, but on the whole they are much smaller than those on Early Lowbush Blueberry. The leaves are oblong or elliptical green and non-hairy on both sides. (Perhaps new leaves may have a slight hairiness on the midvein beneath.) The margins have very fine, bristle-tipped teeth.

The barrel-shaped flower is usually constricted at the throat. It is usually milk-white, but is sometimes tinged with pink. The blossoms are arranged in small clusters along the stem. The very sweet blueberries are similar to *V. vacillans* above. They are nearly black with a heavy bloom. The green warty branches are not hairy, though new growth may have minute hairs at first.

HIGHBUSH BLUEBERRY
Vaccinium corymbosum L.
Heath Family

This blueberry is a tall, compact shrub which may be as tall as fifteen feet. It has spreading branches and is very common in swamps or moist soil, but is also found on dry uplands.

The leaves are 1-3 inches (4-8 cm.) long and come to a very sharp point. Usually the margins are toothless, but some of the leaves may have fine teeth. The lower surface of the leaf is quite often hairy — especially on the veins.

The bright white or pink-tinged flowers are in short racemes at the tips of branches. Each flower is barrel-shaped, constricted at the throat, and has five recurved tips. The flower buds are plump, red, and pointed.

The fruit is a blue-black, smooth, sweet, juicy berry which ripens in late July or August. The fruit is of fine quality for eating, and this blueberry is grown commercially.

The twigs are often reddish. Where the newer twigs are attached to the branchlets, there are brownish, tooth-like appendages encircling the joint. Leaf buds are pointed and have prominent scales and a spine-like tip.

NEW JERSEY BLUEBERRY
Vaccinium caesariense Mackenz.
(not shown)
Heath Family

This bluebery is similar in habit and range to *V. atrococcum,* but is not as common in New England. It grows in bogs, swamps, and peaty thickets chiefly on the coastal plain from southern Maine southward. The dull green leaves are nearly smooth, mostly less than 2 inches (3-5 cm.) in length and have a very short leaf stalk. The corolla is dull white and about ¼ inch (4-6 mm.) long. The berries are dark blue with a bloom and about ¼ inch (5-8 mm.) in diameter. The shrub has many branches and reaches heights up to 10 feet (3 m.).

undeveloped
leaves

BLACK HIGHBUSH BLUEBERRY
Vaccinium atrococcum (Gray) Heller
Heath Family

This blueberry is similar to the Highbush Blueberry but the berry is a shiny violet *black with no bloom.* It grows in swamps and moist woodlands to heights of 3-10 feet.

The oval leaves are dark green above and a lighter green and densely hairy beneath. They *unfold after the flowers* bloom, whereas the leaves are well developed at flowering time on Highbush Blueberry. The calyx lobes are blunt or rounded. The barrel-shaped corolla is yellowish or greenish white tinged with purple. The branches are green and have tiny warts on them. The young twigs are hairy. The berries are polished black without any bloom.

reduced plant

MOUNTAIN CRANBERRY; CROWBERRY; or LINGEN BERRY

Vaccinium vitis-idaea L. var. *minus*, Lodd.
Heath Family

This small spreading cranberry grows in bogs and on wet or dry mossy, rocky slopes to a height of from two to seven inches. The leaves and fruit get much smaller at higher elevations. The stem is quite woody and has small, oval, evergreen glossy-green leaves with tiny black dots on the underside of the leaf. There are only a few pink or white variegated flowers in a small, tight, terminal cluster. Each flower has four petals which are joined together about halfway from the base. Each petal is puffed outward — not restricted at the throat or curved backwards as the flowers of other Heath Family plants. The fruit is a small red berry, acid and slightly bitter. It matures in late summer and makes a delicious cranberry sauce, but the berry will also winter over and is superior in taste in the spring if gathered just as snow is melting.

reduced plant

SMALL CRANBERRY

Vaccinium oxycoccos L.
Heath Family

Small Cranberry grows in cold, wet bogs and wet ground. It has slender erect stems and horizontal rooting stems from 6-18 inches long. The tiny leaves are about ¼ inch long. They are rather thick, evergreen, and are *pointed at the tips*. The margins are rolled over (revolute) and the undersurface of the leaf is white. From one to four slender stalks spring *from the tips of the branch*. Nodding pink flowers hang from these slender stalks. The corolla is divided nearly to the base into 4-5 lobes which fold back over the calyx. The immature berry is pale and sometimes speckled, but becomes red when ripe. It is about 1/3 inch in 'diameter and ripens in August and September.

LARGE CRANBERRY
Vaccinium macrocarpon Ait.
Heath Family

This is the common cranberry of the markets, but it does grow wild in New England bogs. It is similar to the Small Cranberry but is stouter and larger (6-17 mm. long) and the *leaves are rounded at the tips*, not pointed. The leaves are mostly flat and are pale underneath. The flower stalks *do not rise from the tip* as they do on Small Cranberry, but begin midway on the stem. The flower stalk has two leaf-like bracts which are above the middle of the stalk. The corolla is light pink with four petals which turn backwards so far that they often overlap each other. The red and yellow stamens protrude from the center of the flower to form a "beak". The fruit may be oblong or nearly round. It ripens in September and October and is widely used in cooking and for sauce and juice.

a single plant

DIAPENSIA
Diapensia lapponica L.
Diapensia Family

Dispensia is a small woody plant. Many plants grow close together to form low, leafy, evergreen mats on rocks of alpine areas of high mountains. The mat is usually less than four inches tall, and on some mountains may be reduced to look almost moss-like. The base of the plants are pressed together in a brown mass, and only the uppermost leaves are green. The flat, blunt, unlobed leaves are less than ½ inch long. Pretty white flowers rise above the leafy mats in the spring. The corolla is a white, erect bell with five rounded lobes. The five yellow-tipped stamens are attached between the lobes of the flower. When the petals fall, the tan sepals containing the brown seed pod remain in an upright position. At this stage, Diapensia appears to have a small, tan flower on a short stalk rising above the matted leaves.

PERSIMMON
Diospyros virginiana L.
Ebony Family

Persimmon is a medium-sized tree usually 25-50 feet tall, but it reaches heights up to 100 feet near the Mississippi River. Persimmon has a short trunk and a broad crown. It is not found in northern New England. It grows in Connecticut, but is primarily a southern tree.

The simple, alternate leaves have a pointed tip, untoothed margins, and a wedge-shaped to heart-shaped base. They are from 3-7 inches long, dark green and shiny on the upper surface and often hairy below. They are rather thick.

The male and female flowers occur separately. The male ones are in clusters of 2-3 and the female flowers are solitary on stalks in the axils of the leaves. The fruit is a smooth, round, edible fruit which does not ripen until after there has been a frost or some cold weather. The dried calyx remains on the fruit. The ripe fruit is yellowish to reddish and will cling to the tree long after the leaves have fallen.

Bark of older trees is ruggedly corrugated and separates into thick, squarish blocks which will peel off in thin scales. The twigs are slender, bitter, grayish to reddish-brown but become darker the second year. The twigs have pale hairs on them, a few scattered orange-colored marks (lenticels) and a large pith. Winter buds are small, oval-pointed and covered by two dark, glossy scales. There is no true terminal bud.

The wood is heavy, hard, compact, strong, and takes a high polish. It is used for furniture, golf club heads, billiard cues, mallets, parquet flooring, and veneer in states where is it plentiful. Persimmon is not common enough in New England to be of commercial importance in our area.

reduced

233

WHITE ASH
Fraxinus americana L.
Olive Family

White Ash is a large, valuable timber tree usually from 60-80 feet in height. It is a straight-trunked tree which grows best in rich, moist soil. White Ash is common along streams, near lakes and ponds, and in moist woods of lowlands. In winter it is distinguished by the leaf scars with new buds set into a *deep V-shaped notch*.

The opposite, smooth, compound leaves have from five to nine leaflets. The leaflets may be up to five inches long; may have smooth or sparsely-toothed margins; and may or may not be hairy on the underside. Each leaflet is on a short but *distinct stalk* attached to the mid-rib of the compound leaf. Leaves turn purple in the fall.

Male and female flowers appear on different trees. They are small, dark-colored, and appear in clusters in May before the leaves are fully out.

Clusters of long, narrow fruit appear in the late summer and fall. Each fruit has a long, narrow wing at the tip of the seed-bearing portion. The seed-bearing part is cigar-shaped and round in cross-section. The place where the seed ends and the wing begins *is very distinct*.

The bark on young trees is smooth, dark gray or gray brown. Bark on mature trees is divided by diamond-shaped fissures into rather flat, narrow ridges covered with close-fitting scales. The stout twigs are opposite, shiny, smooth, and hairless. The leaf buds are stout, rusty to dark brown or sometimes nearly black. They have blunt points and visible scales.

The wood is heavy, hard, strong, and is valuable for furniture, sporting goods, oars, ax handles, etc.

cigar shaped

Whole leaf may be 15 inches long.

winter bud and leaf scar

234

RED or GREEN ASH
Fraxinus pennsylvanica Marsh.
Olive Family

Red Ash is a medium-sized tree from 30-60 feet tall. It grows along bodies of water and prefers rich soil in valleys. It is similar to White Ash, but the new branchlets have velvety hairs. The leaf stalks, the axis of the compound leaf, and the lower leaf surfaces all have *tawny hairs* on them. The leaves have from 5-9 leaflets which have a point, but gradually narrow at the base. The leaflet blade *extends downward along the upper half of the short stalk on each leaflet* to form a sort of wing. The blade on the White Ash leaflets do not do this. The margins of the leaflets are toothed, but may be entire below the middle. The mature samaras are brownish with the wing portion flanking the seed-bearing part for about half the length. The seed-bearing part is funnel-shaped. It is very *difficult to tell where the seed-body leaves off and the wing begins.* The terminal winter bud is broadly conical and is covered by brownish scales which are visible to the naked eye. The grayish twigs may be either hairy or smooth. The inner layer of epidermis is cinnamon-colored. The wood of Red Ash is heavy, hard, strong, and brittle. It is of lower quality than White Ash and makes a poor firewood.

greatly reduced

samara

235

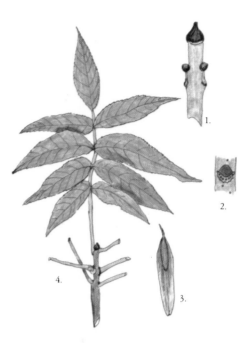

1. winter buds
2. leaf scar
3. samara
4. greatly reduced leaf

BLACK ASH

Fraxinus nigra Marsh.
Olive Family

Black Ash is a small to medium-sized tree usually 60-80 feet in height but occasionally taller, and much smaller when found growing in bogs. Black Ash grows in wet borders of bogs and swamps, along shores, and in other cool, swampy habitats. It seldom thrives on dry land. The bark is thin, gray, flaky, and corky. Rubbing the bark will break it up into a very fine powder. Twigs are rather stout and may be hairy when young, but soon become smooth. *The terminal bud is black*, sharp pointed, and is covered with 1-2 visible bud scales. The first pair of lateral buds are some distance below the terminal bud. The opposite, compound leaves are about 14 inches long with 7-9 *unstalked leaflets* — except for the end one which has a definite stalk. The leaflets have pointed tips, toothed margins, and a wedge-shaped base. A pad of tawny hairs crosses the midrib at the axis of the leaflets. Leaf scars are cresent shaped with numerous bundle scars present. The fruit is a samara with an elliptical, nearly-flat seed body with a wing which extends to the base. (White and Red Ash samara have wings which do not continue to the base of the seed body.) The samara is blunt at both ends.

Black Ash wood is medium in weight, harness and strength. It is comparatively soft and the annual layers are easily separated. It is not a good quality of wood, but it has been used for baskets, barrel hoops, and interior finish of homes.

COMMON LILAC
Syringa vulgaris L.
Olive Family

fruit
pods

This is the only lilac which has escaped and become naturalized. The oval-pointed leaves are 2-5 inches long and have untoothed margins. They abruptly come to an end at the base or may be heart-shaped. The leaf stalk is long and slender. There are numerous flowers in a cluster, and the buds are purple before opening. The funnel-shaped corolla has a long throat and four spreading lobes at the tip. The green calyx is a small and four lobed. When the flowers open, they are pale lavender and are very fragrant. The bark gets shaggy on larger shrubs. This lilac will spread by means of underground shoots.

PRIVET or PRIM
Ligustrum vulgare L.
Olive Family

Privet is a tall shrub up to 16 feet high (5 m.) with gray-brown twigs with white "warts". The branchlets may be smooth or minutely hairy. This shrub was introduced from Europe but has escaped and become established in open woods or thickets. The twigs are very leafy with opposite, deciduous leaves. The firm, dark green leaves are long and narrowed at both ends. Usually they are less than 3 inches (3-6 cm.) long, but on shrubs growing where it is unusually rich, may be as long as 4 inches. The fruit is a hard, nearly round berry. It is shiny black and arranged in clusters. The small white barrel-shaped flowers are in clusters at the tips of branchlets. The winter buds are small and tan-colored with visible scales.

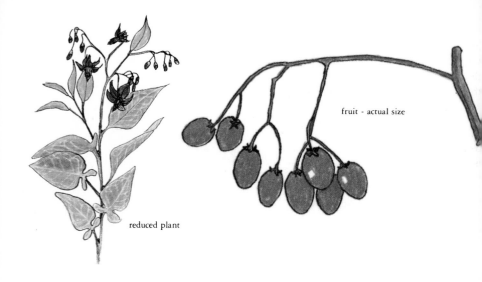

fruit - actual size

reduced plant

CLIMBING NIGHTSHADE or BITTERSWEET
Solanum dulcamara L.
Nightshade Family

Bittersweet — also called Purple Nightshade — is a weak climbing or reclining vine-like plant which grows in moist thickets throughout our area. The stem is often as long as six or eight feet. The flowers are similar to those of the common potato. The five swept-back violet petals surround the orange beak-like center. The top leaves are simple and pointed, but the larger lower leaves have two small lobes at the base. The fruit is a red, egg-shaped berry which is borne in drooping clusters. Both the foliage and the berries are mildly poisonous.

SOUTHERN CATALPA or CATAWBA TREE
Catalpa bignonioides Walt.
Bignonia Family

This catalpa tree is nearly 100 feet tall in its natural western habitat, but is not that tall when found in New England. This tree is an introduced species. It survives in New England, but rarely escapes.

The broad leaves with a heart-shaped base taper to an abrupt point. They are 6-12 inches long and emit a *strong odor when bruised*. Catalpa leaves are bright green and smooth above, but may be hairy beneath.

The flowers are 1-1½ inches long and are arranged in pyramidal clusters. Each flower is two-lipped, has two yellow stripes and is conspicuously dotted on the inner surface with brown-purple spots.

The mature fruit is a long, bean-like capsule up to 20 inches in length — many occurring together in a cluster. The mature fruit has a thick wall and is about ¼ inch in diameter at the middle. The wings of the seeds inside have a fringe of short hairs at the ends.

The bark is red-brown and is broken into thin scales. The wood is very durable, but is not commercially used in New England. This tree is largely planted as a lawn tree.

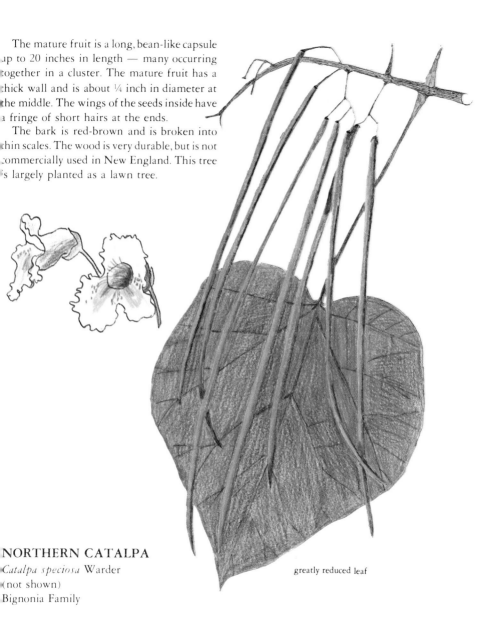

greatly reduced leaf

NORTHERN CATALPA

Catalpa speciosa Warder
(not shown)
Bignonia Family

This species is similar to the above, but it has larger fruits which are ½ to ¾ inch in diameter. The bruised *leaves emit no odor.*

PARTRIDGE-BERRY or RUNNING BOX
Mitchella repens L.
Madder Family

Partridge-Berry is a low, creeping evergreen herb which grows on dry or moist knolls in woods. The paired evergreen leaves are small, nearly round, and often variegated with whitish veins.

The pink or white flowers have a tubular throat and four spreading petals which are hairy on the inside. The paired flowers are joined together at the base because they have united ovaries. The fuit which develops from the united ovaries is a single red (occasionally white) berry-like drupe which is edible but rather tasteless. The "berry" *has two blossom ends* instead of only one as most other berries do. The "berry" is firm and will remain on the plant all winter if not eaten by wildlife. This plant makes an excellent plant to put in woodland terrariums — especially if a plant with berries on it can be found.

BUTTONBUSH
Cephalanthus occidentalis L.
Madder Family

Buttonbush is an erect shrub up to 6 feet in height. It grows in wet soil of swamps, bogs, and along borders of ponds and streams.

The leaves are opposite, or in whorls of three or four which originate at the same point on the stem. Sometimes there are triangular

stipules at the leaf axils, or between the whorls of leaves. The leaf blades are rounded at the base, pointed at the tip, have untoothed margins, and are on short but distinct leaf stalks.

The white flowers are in dense, spherical heads about one inch in diameter. These appear in July. The individual flowers are long and tubular with four petals at the end of the tube. The style protrudes from the throat of the flower.

The fruit is a round dry ball or button about the same size as the flower head. It contains many small pods and remains on the shrub during the winter.

The small leaf buds are in depressed areas of the stem and are surrounded by outer bark above the circular leaf scars. The pith inside the stem is light brown.

NORTHERN BUSH-HONEYSUCKLE
Diervilla lonicera Mill.
Honeysuckle Family

Northern Bush-Honeysuckle is from one to four feet tall and grows in dry or rocky soil in woods openings or at the edges of fields. This is the only honeysuckle with *toothed leaves*. The leafblades are oblong and pointed at the tip and are opposite each other on the stem. The trumpet-shaped flowers are pale yellow and grow in sets of twos or threes from the leaf axils and at the tips of the stems. The stamens protrude noticeably, and the petals fold way back.

MOUNTAIN-FLY HONEYSUCKLE
Lonicera villosa (Michx.) R. & S.
Honeysuckle Family

This honeysuckle is a low shrub — rarely as tall as 3 feet — with strongly ascending branches and hairy twigs. It grows in peaty or rocky barrens and in bogs.

The leaves are variable. They are oval but the base may be rounded or narrowed. They usually have a blunt tip and little or no leaf stalk. The leaf is hairy on both surfaces and has a conspicuous fine network of veins. The flowers are yellowish or straw-colored. They are tubular with five almost equal lobes but are *not two-lobed* as are the flowers on Swamp Fly Honeysuckle. The fruit is an edible berry. It is a two-eyed berry consisting of two ovaries surrounded by juicy pulp. The skin is blue with a whitish bloom.

LY HONEYSUCKLE

onicera xylosteum L.

oneysuckle Family

hollow twigs

Fly Honeysuckle is similar to Morrow's oneysuckle. Read the descriptions of both efore making an identification. This oneysuckle has been planted and has casionally escaped to thickets, roadsides or sturbed woods where it may reach heights o to 9 feet. It is similar to *L. morrowi* but is a ore bushy shrub with *hollow branches* and ght brown, hairy twigs. The leaves are liptical or sometimes have the broadest part ove the middle. The base may be rounded or oadly wedge-shaped. Leaves are usually less an 2½ inches (3-6 cm.) and are smooth and ay-green above and are pale with downy irs on the underside. Leaf stalks are hairy. The flowers are in pairs on thread-like, iry stalks which rise from the axils of the aves. The *flower is strongly two-lipped* with e upper three petals fused together nearly to e tip. The corolla is about ½ inch (1 cm.) ng and may be whitish, yellowish, or even nkish. The bracts at the base of the pair of wers are much shorter than those on *L. orrowi* — usually less than one half the ngth of the ovary. The red berries are stinct and are *not united at the base*. Winter ds are elongated and pointed, and the scales ar long hairs on the margins.

MORROW'S HONEYSUCKLE

Lonicera morrowi Gray
Honeysuckle Family

L. morrowi is similar to *L. xylosteum* and
the differences will be noted in the text. This
honeysuckle has divergent branches. It is a
native of Eurasia, and in America it has usually
escaped from cultivation to roadsides and
thickets.

The flowers on *L. morrowi* are a little larger
than on *L. xylosteum* and are not two-lipped.
The corolla is white and soon becomes
creamy-yellow. The petals are separate for
about 1/2 to 2/3 of their length. The stalks
which hold the paired flowers have soft hairs.
These stalks are ¼ to ⅝ inch (.5-1.5 cm.) long.
The hairy bracts at the base of the paired
flowers are at least half as long and usually
longer than the length of the ovary. These
bracts are much shorter on *L. xylosteum*.
When the fruit is forming, this pair of long
slender bracts is quite noticeable at the base of
each pair of red or yellow berries. *Berries are
united at the base.* The leaves are oblong to
narrow-oval and are 1-2 inches (2.5-5 cm.) in
length. The undersides of the leaf blades are
densely hairy with gray hairs, and the leaf
stalks and the new twigs are also hairy. Winter
buds on *L. morrowi* are small, blunt, and
nearly hairless, while winter buds on *L.
xylosteum* are long, pointed and have scales
with hairs on the margins.

hollow

TARTARIAN HONEYSUCKLE
Lonicera tatarica L.
Honeysuckle Family

This honeysuckle is an upright shrub up to 10 or 12 feet in height. It is a native of Europe, but has been frequently planted as an ornamental in New England. It has escaped and has become naturalized in thickets, open woods, and along roadsides.

The opposite leaves are thin and hairless — or nearly so. The leaves are simple and are dark green above and light green to bluish green beneath.

The two-lipped pink (or white) *tubular flowers are in pairs.* The base of the flower is swollen and there are five spreading, petal-like divisions at the tip of the tube. The flowers usually open in May.

The fruit is usually red, but occasionally it is yellow. The berries are *united at the base* and are on a common stalk about an inch long.

Tartarian Honeysuckle has smooth twigs with hollow centers. The bark on older branches is gray, but bark on branchlets is brown.

AMERICAN FLY-HONEYSUCKLE
Lonicera canadensis Bartr.
Honeysuckle Family

Fly Honeysuckle is a straggling, loosely-branched shrub from 2-5 feet high. It is quite common in rocky or cool woods and thickets. The branchlets are smooth and light brown.

The opposite leaves are smooth on both surfaces. The blade is oblong to egg-shaped and is on a short, *hairy leaf stalk*. The base of the leaf blade varies from rounded to heart-shaped. Some leaves have hair on the margins.

The pale yellow or greenish-yellow flowers are borne in paris on a common flower stalk about an inch long. Each flower is narrowly funnel-shaped and has five pointed lobes at the tip. There is a bulge on one side at the base of the tubular corolla.

The fruit is a handsome, elongated red berry. The berries are separate, but *in pairs* on a common stalk. The berries point outward from their bases.

SWAMP-FLY HONEYSUCKLE
Lonicera oblongifolia (Goldie) Hook.
Honeysuckle Family

This honeysuckle grows in acid bogs, White Cedar swamps, or wet thickets and woods to heights up to five feet. It resembles Fly Honeysuckle, but the leaves on this shrub have fine hairs underneath and the twigs have a *solid white pith* instead of a hollow pith.

The opposite leaves are somewhat oblong, from 1-3 inches long. The lower side of the leaf is minutely downy and conspicuously veined. The two-lipped flowers are yellowish-white. They open in late May and are arranged in pairs on long stalks rising from the leaf axils. The fruits are red or orange-yellow berries which grow in pairs and may be distinct or united. The twigs are light brown with soft hairs on them.

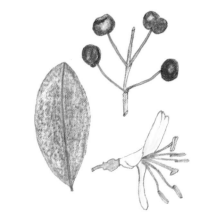

JAPANESE HONEYSUCKLE
Lonicera japonica Thunb.
Honeysuckle Family

Japanese Honeysuckle is an introduced, high-twining or trailing hairy shrub or vine which — once established — will form dense tangles where it climbs over underbrush and sprawls on the ground. It grows in thickets and borders of woods and old fields where it may strangle out the native plants. Once established, it is a difficult weed to eradicate.

The honeysuckle is similar to the others in this book, but the *berries are black* and the *upper leaves are not united.* The leaves are in pairs, but each has its own distinct stalk. The leaves are rather thick, ovate or oblong and have untoothed margins. They are green on both sides, or some may be purplish-green underneath. Some of the lower leaves may be lobed.

The tubular white or white-tinged-with-purple flowers often become yellow with age. They are in pairs in the axils of the upper leaves. Below each pair of flowers is a pair of small leaf-like, green bracts. The flowers are from ½ to 1 inch long, have a hairy tube, and are very fragrant.

The older branches are brown. Newer growth is often densely hairy.

TRUMPET or
CORAL HONEYSUCKLE

Lonicera sempervirens L.
Honeysuckle Family

This honeysuckle is a high climbing o
twining vine with a smooth, *hollow stem.* I
grows in woods and thickets where it may
have escaped from cultivation. The firm, semi
evergreen oblong leaves are in pairs. The
upper *pairs are joined together* in a disk
around the stem. The leaves are usually
hairless — but may have minute hairs on the
underside. They are green on top but whitish
underneath.

The coral-red flowers are mostly in whorls
of 2-4. Each flower has a long, slender, tubular
throat which is red on the outside and has
nearly equal, short, rounded lobes which are
yellowish on the inside. The stamens and style
may extend slightly from the throat of the
flower. The fruit is a red berry.

TWINING HONEYSUCKLE

Lonicera dioica L.
Honeysuckle Family

This honeysuckle is rarely found in
northern New England, but is more common
in southern New England where it grows on
ledges, in dry woods and thickets, or along
river banks. It is a twining or sprawling shrub
which resembles Trumpet Honeysuckle. The
shrub is essentially hairless, has woody, light
brown stems, and the larger, older stems have

gray, shreddy bark. The uppermost pairs of leaves are joined into one. The united leaf has narrow to blunt points with an indentation mid-way on the margins. The lower leaves are oblong or elliptic and may have a short stalk or be attached directly to the twig. There is a *waxy, whitish covering* on the underside of the leaf. Flowers are usually in small whorls of 1-3, but the cluster at the tip of the twig usually contains more. The flowers may be yellowish to dark red and are *strongly two-lipped*. They are smooth on the outside but are hairy within. The corolla tube is usually swollen at the base on one side only. The berries are red.

HAIRY HONEYSUCKLE

Lonicera hirsuta Eat.
Honeysuckle Family

This twining and high climbing honeysuckle has glandular hairs on the branchlets. It grows in moist woods, on bluffs, and along limy shores. The broadly-oval leaves have stiff, straight hairs and soft hairs on the upper surface. The stiff hairs are especially noticeable along the edges of the leaves. The under surface has downy hairs and the veins are very prominent. The deep green leaves are paired, and the upper leaves are joined to form a single disk around the stem. The yellow to orange flowers are in whorls. The flowers are sticky-hairy on the outside and the inside of the throat is also hairy. Each tubular flower is 1-1½ inches long and has a slightly enlarged base. The fruit is a cluster of red berries.

SNOWBERRY
Symphoricarpos albus (L.) Blake or
   Symphoricarpos racemosus Michx.
Honeysuckle Family

Snowberry is a small shrub 1-3 feet in height with slender branches and shreddy bark. It is native to limy ledges and gravels, but a cultivated variety *laevigatus* has spread to roadsides and ledges. The slender branchlets are hollow. The soft, thin leaves are oval or nearly round and are 1-2 inches long. Margins are usually toothless, but on young shoots the leaves may be toothed. The small bell-shaped flowers are pinkish on the outside and hairy inside, about ¼ inch long and have five lobes. They may be in terminal clusters of from 5-20 or in small axillary clusters of 1-5. The waxy, white fruit is a depressed globe when mature and is very conspicuous in the early winter. Fruits usually form in the axils, but some may be in a terminal cluster.

TWINFLOWER
Linnaea borealis L.
   var. *americana* (Forbes) Rehd.
Honeysuckle Family

Twinflower is a slender, creeping or trailing evergreen which grows in cool woods and on peaty knolls of bogs. The paired leaves are yellow-green in color. They are rounded with obscure teeth on the margins. The flowers grow in pairs and nod from the tips of forking, thread-like, upright flower stalks. Each fragrant flower is funnel-shaped and about ½ inch long. The corolla is pale pink or tinged with rose, has five lobes and is hairy on the inside. There is a five-toothed calyx at the base of each flower.

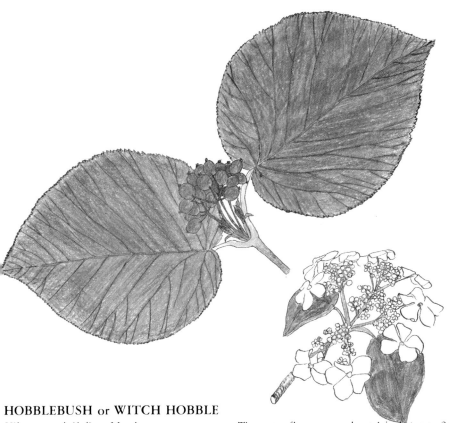

HOBBLEBUSH or WITCH HOBBLE

Viburnum alnifolium Marsh.
Honeysuckle Family

Hobblebush is a straggling, irregular shrub from 3-8 feet high. The arching stems may take root and new shrubs will grow to form dense thickets. This shrub is common in lowlands, cool and moist woods, on shores of ponds, and along streams.

The large, opposite leaves are nearly round. They have finely-toothed margins and a heart-shaped base. Rusty hairs are on the underside of the leaves and on the leaf stalks.

The flowers are in large white (rarely pink) clusters. The outer rim of flowers is large and showy, but these have no reproductive parts.

The outer flowers are about 1 inch (up to 2.5 cm.) broad, but the true flowers on the inside of the cluster are much smaller. Both types of flowers have a corolla with five rounded lobes.

The fruit is a berry-like drupe about 1/3 inch long, and is tipped with a brown dot. The fruit changes from red to nearly black at maturity. It develops in August, but remains on the shrub late into the fall.

Winter buds are conspicuous and consist of two small, rusty-brown leaves enclosing a compact flower bud. Branches are slender and tough. Young twigs are rough scurfy or hairy. The bark is a dull madder purple or brown and is smooth. The twigs and buds are a favorite food for deer.

WITHEROD or WILD RAISIN

Viburnum cassinoides L.
Honeysuckle Family

Witherod is a slender, erect shrub from 2-15 feet tall. It grows in clearings, swamps or bogs, moist thickets and in lowlands. The opposite leaves are variable — even on the same plant. Some may have small, obscure teeth while others have only wavy margins. The leaves are oval or elliptical, are on leaf stalks, and have pointed tips. The leaves are green and rather thick and leathery. They are smooth on both sides but somewhat scurfy on the veins underneath.

The ill-scented white flowers are only 1/5 inch (5 mm.) broad. They are arranged in dome-shaped clusters 2-4 inches (3-10 cm.) across. The anthers are elevated above the center of the flower and give a feathery appearance to the cluster. Flowers bloom in June and July.

The fruit is a ½ inch long berry-like drupe with dry, sweet pulp and a flat stone. It develops in August but stays on until late in the fall. It is whitish or yellow at first, then turns pink, and eventually bluish-black at maturity.

The branches and stems are rather scurfy. The stems are brownish gray and the branches are a light, warm brown. Winter buds are covered by a single pair of yellow or golden scurfy rabbit-ear-like scales.

reduced

SWAMP or POSSUM HAW
Viburnum nudum L.
Honeysuckle Family

Possum Haw — also called Larger Witherod — is a coarser and more tree-like shrub than *V. cassinoides* and grows in southern New England only. It may be tree-like with a trunk 4-8 inches (1-2 dm.) in diameter and up to 18 or 20 feet (6 m.) in height, or be a spreading or straggling shrub. Young shoots are green or merely dotted. Possum Haw grows in wooded swamps, wet pinelands and bogs. The opposite, leathery leaves are lustrous above. The leaf tip may be rounded, but it does not taper to a narrow point. There is a hairiness on the stalks at the axils of leaves on new growth. Leaves on fertile branches may be up to 6 inches (6-15 cm.) long. Margins have fine rounded teeth, but may be rolled under and appear toothless. The fruit is a blue, nearly-round drupe with bitter flesh and a round-oval stone inside. The flowers are in a broad cluster on brownish stalks. The anthers are elevated above the throat of the corolla. Winter buds are brown or gray brown.

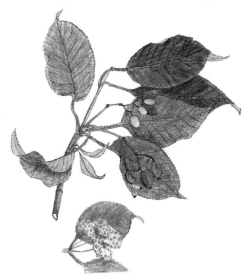

NANNYBERRY,
SWEET VIBURNUM,
WILD RAISIN
Viburnum lentago L.
Honeysuckle Family

Nannyberry is a large shrub or small tree up to 25 feet in height. It is very showy in early June when it is in bloom, and can be found along roads at borders of woods, on stream banks or in thickets. It resembles Witherod, but the *leaves are finely and evenly toothed* and abruptly come to a point. The opposite leaves have leaf stalks with margins that are wavy or toothed.

The flowers are in clusters 2-5 inches across, but the cluster usually *lacks any main stem.* Each tiny flower has five spreading white petals, five white stamens with golden yellow tips, and a green ovary in the center. The edible fruit has sweet pulp and a large stone inside. It is blue-black in color when it matures in September.

twig and
enlarged buds

BLACK or SWEET HAW
Viburnum prunifolium L.
Honeysuckle Family

Black Haw is a shrub or small tree usually not taller than 15 feet, but occasionally reaching heights up to 35 feet. The short trunk — often crooked — bears a rather broad, round-topped crown. Black Haw grows in southern New England and southward on dry, rocky hillsides, along fences, and in thickets. Mature bark is reddish-brown and rough, and is broken into thick plate-like scales. Newer twigs are smooth and reddish at first, then turn green and later gray with a film-like bloom. The twigs usually have orange-colored marks. The simple, opposite leaves are 1-3 inches long, are slightly pointed and have a wedge-shaped base. They are dark green on top and pale green below and are apt to get leathery as they mature. The margins may have fine teeth and the round leaf stalks may be winged. Small white flowers appear in May in dense terminal clusters 3-4 inches broad. The green fruit is a shiny, hard, flattened oval drupe with a projection at the tip. The mature fruit is a sweet, juicy, dark blue drupe with a flat, oval stone. Fruits are in clusters borne on reddish stalks.

DOWNY ARROWWOOD
Viburnum rafinesquianum Schultes
Honeysuckle Family

   This arrowwood is rare in southern New Hampshire, more common in the Champlain area of Vermont, and has not been found growing in Maine. It may be more common in southern New England, and grows in open woods and on dry slopes, low grounds, or barrens. It may be a straggling or a dense shrub up to 6 feet (2 m.) in height. This arrowwood resembles *V. recognitum,* but may be distinguished from it by the soft hairs on the underside of the leaf and the short leaf stalks. *V. recognitum* has leaf stalks ½-1¼ inches (3 cm.) long, while this one may have a very short stalk or be attached directly to the twig. The branchlets are smooth and pale. The winter buds have 2 pairs of outer scales. The pair of leaves immediately below the stalk holding the flower cluster will have a pair of long stipules. Leaf blades are 1¼ to 3¼ inches (3-8 cm.) long and are somewhat heart-shaped with coarsely-toothed margins. The solid fruit is dark purple, elliptical and is less than ⅜ inch (7-9 mm.) broad.

NORTHERN ARROWWOOD
Viburnum recognitum Fern.
Honeysuckle Family

This arrowwood is an erect shrub 3-9 feet in height. It has many branches, with the older branches being straight and arrow-like, and grows in moist woods and damp thickets, and along shores.

The opposite leaves are nearly round in outline, but have prominent, coarse teeth. They are from 1-3 inches (3-9 cm.) long. Veins on the upper surface are indented, and they are very prominent on the underside of the leaf. The leaves are hairless and may be slightly heart-shaped at the base.

The small white flowers are in flat clusters from 2-4 inches across. The flowers bloom in June. The deep blue to black fruit is a berry 1/3 inch long which develops in August. The berries are in a long-stemmed cyme and the stalks are tinged with red. The stone inside the berry is deeply grooved.

The twigs are hairless and often somewhat 6-sided or ridged.

basal leaf and
a single flower

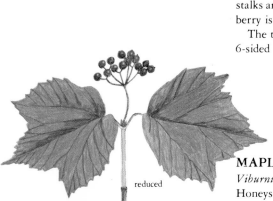

reduced

MAPLE-LEAVED VIBURNUM
Viburnum acerifolium L.
Honeysuckle Family

Maple-Leaved Viburnum is a slender, branched shrub 2-6 feet high. It has smooth, warm gray or dull brown stem and branches, and grows in dry or rocky woods.

The opposite leaves are 3-lobed and resemble a maple leaf. They may be up to five inches (4-12 cm.) broad and are very soft-downy and dotted on the underside. In autumn the leaves turn pink or purple.

The flowers are in a white cluster 1½ to 3½ inches (2-9 cm.) across on a long, slender stalk. The flowers are small — about ¼ inch broad — with prominent stamens. They appear in June.

The fruit is round with a nipple-like tip. At first it is reddish, but it turns purple-black as it matures. Winter buds are opposite and have two pairs of bud scales.

SQUASHBERRY or MOOSEBERRY
Viburnum edule (Michx.) Raf.
Honeysuckle Family

Squashberry is a straggling shrub from 6 inches to 6 feet in height which grows on cool slopes or ravines of northern New England. The branchlets are ridged smooth and reddish-brown — especially towards the tip. Winter buds have 2 outer scales and are deep maroon in color. The older leaves have three shallow lobes, while the end leaves are usually unlobed. The yellow-green leaves are leathery and the veins on the top surface look "sunken in". The margins are coarsely toothed, and the leaf blade has from 3-5 main nerves which originate at the base. The milk-white flowers are in small, dense clusters ½ to 1¼ inches wide. All of the flowers are fertile, and there is no ring of larger sterile ones around the edge of the cluster as there is on the Highbush Cranberry. The immature fruit is a yellow drupe, but it becomes red, sour and juicy at maturity. It is edible and is used to make jam. The stone inside is flattened.

HIGHBUSH CRANBERRY

Viburnum trilobum Marsh.
Honeysuckle Family

Highbush Cranberry is a tall shrub which reaches heights to 12 feet, with smooth, nearly erect branches. It grows in moist or swampy woods and on alluvial plains.

The opposite leaves are 3-lobed, but the *bottom third is without teeth* and the top part has only a few teeth. Sometimes the leaves are broader than they are long. The red leaf stalks are long and grooved, and bear round-tipped hairs (glands) near the junction of the blades. Leaf blades are distinctly *three-ribbed at the base.*

The flowers are in large white clusters — the outer rim of flowers are enlarged and showy, but sterile. These flowers have five petals, are about one inch broad, and appear in June.

The fruit is bright red, almost ½ inch long, and is in conspicuous clusters. It ripens in August, is edible but sour, and has a flat, ungrooved stone. The fruit is used for preserves, jelly, and cranberry sauce. The fruit clusters hang down when ripe.

The winter buds are opposite, plump and smooth. They are in axils of leaves and have two scales. The stem of the twigs is angled or ridged.

GUELDER-ROSE
Viburnum opulus L.
Honeysuckle Family

Guelder-Rose is very similar to Highbush Cranberry, but the leaves are more rounded in general outline with less prolonged lobes. It is frequently planted and has occasionally escaped. The top surface of the leaf is dark green with sunken veins. The bottom surface is lighter in color and has a prominent network of veins. At the base of the leaf stalk are thread-like stipules. Below the base of each leaf blade on the petiole is a pair of green mushroom-shaped glands with saucer-shaped tops. The flower cluster is similar to that of Highbush Cranberry. The fruit is less pleasant to taste than that of the Highbush Cranberry, and in some instances is very bitter. The young green twigs are ribbed and have tiny brown warts on them. Older twigs are gray-brown with many light-colored warts.

SNOWBALL TREE
Viburnum opulus var. *roseum* L.
(not shown)
Honeysuckle Family

Snowball Tree is a variety of the species described above. It is very similar, but the flower cluster is more rounded, and all the flowers are enlarged and sterile.

COMMON ELDER or ELDERBERRY

Sambucus canadensis L.
Honeysuckle Family

Elderberry is a tall shrub with dark maroon or green twigs. These twigs have a large *white sponge-like pith* and have a rank odor when bruised. The shrub is usually 4-8 feet tall, but may reach heights up to 10 feet. The bark of lower branches is gray and warty and there is usually a swelling at the joints. Elderberry is common on rich, moist lowlands and is usually found in thickets or in open places along paths, roadsides or streams.

The opposite compound leaves may have from 5-11 leaflets, 2-5 inches long — usually only 7. Each oval leaflet has an acute point and sharply-toothed margins. Leaflets are green on top, smooth and paler in color underneath. the leaf stalk is yellow green.

Numerous small flowers less than ¼ inch across are in dense, broad, rather flat-topped clusters. Each tiny flower has five prominent stamens. The flowers open in June and July. The fruit is a juicy berry-like drupe which is black-purple when ripe. The "berries" have a bitter taste, but are good for making elderberry wine or jelly. They ripen late in August.

brown
pith

RED BERRIED ELDER
Sambucus pubens Michx.
Honeysuckle Family

Red Berried Elder is a large shrub 10-15 feet tall. It is common throughout northern New England but becomes less common southward. It grows on rocky mountain slopes, in rocky woods and on ledges. The *twigs have a rank odor when bruised,* and brown pith inside.

This elder has from 5-7 oval pointed leaflets. (Common Elderberry has 7-11.) The leaflets have sharply toothed margins and may be downy on the underside. Leaflets are from 2-4 inches long.

Numerous small yellowish-white flowers are in elongated clusters which bloom early in the spring. (Elderberry has flat-topped clusters of flowers which bloom much later.)

The fruit is in a showy, elongated cluster. Each red berry-like drupe contains three small seed-like nutlets. The fruit on this elder is *not edible*, whereas that on Common Elderberry is.

Another identifying characteristic is the brown or orange pith. Common Elderberry has white pith.

The branchlets on this elder are hairy and the bark is warty. The roundish buds may have a purplish tinge and are opposite on the stem.

261

MARSH ELDER or
HIGHWATER SHRUB
Iva frutescens L.
Composite Family

Highwater shrub is really a sub-shrub as only the base is woody. Though it reaches heights up to three feet, it dies back each winter. This variety is found in salt marshes along the coast.

The larger, lower leaves are opposite and have from 6-15 teeth on each margin. The upper leaves are long and narrow and are often alternate. They look almost like narrow bracts under each flower head. The flower heads are nodding, each on its own short, curved stalk rising from the leaf axil. Both male and female flowers develop within each flower cluster.

GROUNDSEL-TREE or
GROUNDSEL-BUSH
Baccharis halimifolia L.
Thistle Family

Groundsel-Tree is a branching, smooth shrub 3-10 feet high. It grows along salt marshes and tidal rivers, but is not found north of Massachusetts.

The spreading, leafy branchlets are angled and may be scurfy. The lower leaves are thick, have stalks, and have a few coarse teeth or pointed lobes. Usually they are alternate, but larger, lower leaves may be nearly opposite. The leaves on the branchlets are smaller; they may be on short stalks or be attached directly to the branchlet. They are usually unlobed, but may have a few teeth at the tip. The tufted flower heads are in stalked clusters of 1-5 in axils of upper leaves. The hairy tufts (pappus) are bright white but may turn tan with age. The cottony clusters of white pappus are very conspicuous in the autumn.

INDEX OF COMMON NAMES

INDEX OF LATIN NAMES